Low Fat and Happy

Flavorful family-style recipes that will leave
you feeling satisfied, not deprived!

by Teresa Collins

Copyright© 1997
Teresa Collins

Aspire Publishing
P.O. Box 392
Chelsea, OK 74016
Printed in the U.S.A.

ISBN 0-9660238-7-0
Library of Congress Catalog Card Number 97-94333

Third Printing - May 1998

Printed by Jumbo Jack's Cookbooks, Audubon,IA 50025

Dedication

This book is lovingly dedicated to the #1 guys in my life: my husband and three sons.

To my best friend and husband Bill. Words are not enough to let you know how much your love and encouragement have meant to me. My dream is now a reality because of you. Thank you for wearing the hat of Mr. Mom during the final stages of our book. The boys and I are truly blessed to have you in our lives. I love you, me.

To Cody. Thank you for becoming my coach. For all the times you sat on my feet and said, "Come on, Mom, one more sit up, you can do it." Your love and help with your brothers is more than any mom could ask for. You are a wonderful son and big brother. I am very proud of you. I love you, Mom.

To Jake. I could always count on you asking, "So, Mom, how was your day?" Your hugs and words of encouragement kept me going. You are my Number One Fishing Buddy. I am very proud of you. I love you, Mom.

To Wyatt. Seeing your eyes light up and giving your mischievous little grin when you saw me for the first time in your life wearing my "skinny clothes" simply melted my heart. You have earned the title as Mom's Number One chef by always being ready to help me try out new recipes. I am very proud of you. I love you, Mom.

Acknowledgments

- **Don Lee Wooldridge** - To my dad, whose ear is never too tired to listen, whose eyes never blink at disappointment, and whose heart has never quit showing just how much he cares. Thanks! I love you Dad for always being there for me.

- **Norma Jean Ashley** - To my mom, who instilled in me at an early age to stand up straight, to be proud of being tall, having freckles and red hair. To remember that "the wings of the bumble bee aren't large enough to allow him to fly... but he does anyway, because no one has told him that he can't" - Norma Jean Ashley. Mom, I love you!

- **Donald Gene Wooldridge** - To my brother, for always challenging me to keep going! Finally, I weigh less than you do! Ha! Ha! Not only are you my brother, you are my good friend. I love you, brother!

- **Delphia Conn** - To my Grandma Conn, the memories of days spent at Grandma's house as a child always bring a smile to my face. Whether it was sitting on a fishing bank with a cold biscuit or smelling the dinner you were fixing as I walked through the gate, I will cherish those memories forever! I love you, Grandma!

- **James (Jim) Conn** - To my beloved Grandpa Conn, who taught me not only to appreciate half-and-half on Grandma's bread puddin', but who also taught me that wishing for it all at once simply takes away from the adventure of it all. I love and miss you, Grandpa!

- **Ethel Wooldridge** - To my beloved Grandma whom I received the love of writing and creating from. I love and miss you!

- **Novel Wooldridge** - To my beloved Grandpa whom I got my love for fishing from. I love and miss you!

- **Denis Curtin** - To someone whose food for thought was just the encouragement I needed! Thank you!

- **Jerry Shaffer** - To my dear friend whose positive outlook on life is always uplifting! Thank you!

- **Janis Wooley** - Your words of honesty and encouragement have helped me more than you will ever know! Thank you!

- **Mary Lewis** - Thank you for listening to me go through the process of losing weight and for never failing to pay a compliment just when I needed it most! Thank you!

- **The Kids on School Bus #7** - You guys are the best group of kids any bus driver could ever ask for. I'm proud to be your bus driver. Thanks for making me laugh and a big hug to all of you for encouraging me to never give up on myself! I love you guys!

- **Family & Friends** - To all those family members and friends whose names do not appear—your words of encouragement will not soon be forgotten! I am truly blessed!

3

Love,
Teresa

Table of Contents

Author's Preface

My story is not so different from anyone else who has experienced a constant battle with weight. I, like so many of you, bear in my heart the emotional scars that being obese brings. I have gone up and down in weight so many times in my life, who counts anymore. Take it from me when I tell you it can be different for us and it's not as hard as you think. You can shed that ball and chain that is holding you back from being the person you've only dreamed of.

Like I stated earlier, I have gone on so many diets in my lifetime where either the food was so bland, the amount so limited, or it tasted like the box it just came out of. I would soon find myself off the diet and again left feeling like a failure. One of the many starvation type diets I went on after my divorce not only left me seventy-five pounds lighter, it left me with less hair on my head. At what cost to me physically did I pay to lose those seventy-five pounds?

I can remember planning very carefully to go on diets—never on my birthday, or anyone else's for that matter! I sure wouldn't want to miss out on the cake and ice cream. Never during the holidays; what would life be like not eating a bountiful harvest or Santa's favorite fixin's? And I always would start them on a Monday. Why, you ask? So I could gorge myself with all my favorite foods I would find myself deprived of once the new diet began.

All of this sounds so crazy to me now, but back then it was just a way of life. Well, not really a life, more like an existence.

With each new diet I went on I just knew that this was going to be the one that would set me free. Wrong. The only thing it freed me of was a few pounds that I would put right back on and then some. And the only thing that was 100% guaranteed with those diets was feeling like a failure.

After years of living this way I found myself weighing more than I ever thought possible, 300 pounds of pure misery. I remember looking at the scales with my heart sinking and asking myself why. Why did I let this happen to me? Were all those candy bars worth it? Was eating as much as I wanted and then some worth it? Was hiding my binges from my family worth it?

Was living with a tingling feeling in the calves of my legs because they were stretched to their limit worth it? Was lying down at night and not being able to breathe comfortably, worth it? Was the looming cloud of heart disease, diabetes, and high blood pressure worth it? Was living with back pain twenty-four hours a day, worth it? Somewhere deep inside me screamed the words, "No! No! No!" I want to live! The person who looked back at me in the mirror then was not me.

More thoughts entered my head, like the thought of leaving my sons and husband at an early age. The thought of not being the active mom that I wanted to be with my boys. The thought of not rocking my grandbabies while sitting with my husband on our porch. The thought of not living anymore terrified me.

That very day—Wednesday—the research began. I took notice of what diets had failed me in the past and how unhappy I was during the whole "diet thing". This time I knew if it was going to work I was going to have to be able to eat and feel satisfied. I knew I had limited amount of time to spend in the kitchen so the meals that I prepared were going to have to satisfy all of us. No more cooking separate meals. I was tired of feeling so deprived with what was on my plate—or more like what wasn't on my plate.

The first step I took was reading the food labels in my kitchen cabinets. After reading the labels, I decided with my past eating habits, no wonder I weighed 300 pounds. It also became very clear to me that I have a responsibility of setting a better example of healthy eating for my sons. To spare them the heartaches that being overweight brings.

Cooking and living the low-fat lifestyle has changed our lives. I say *our* because my husband and boys will be the first to tell you what a happier wife and mom I am now.

I'm proud to say that in 15 months I have lost 120 pounds. I now can outwalk my husband and the boys are the ones saying to me they are tired of playing ball. I'm a new person inside and out. I love to wear pretty clothes and the person that looks back at me in the mirror, now, is me.

The meals I prepare for my family are very satisfying. I can honestly say that I don't miss the skin on my oven fried chicken and desserts just look fattening. I, as well as my family, are very satisfied with the recipes in this book. After all, they have given me my life back. I also love knowing that the tricks of cooking and eating low fat that I have learned will keep me a healthy happy size for life.

So. . . what are you waiting for? I know it sounds simple—cook low fat, be low fat, but it's true. You too can become healthy and happy for life. I'm living proof that these recipes work. If they can work for me, I know they can work for you too. Give yourself another chance. You are worth it! See you in the kitchen. Happy Cooking!

I would love to hear from you.

Write to: Teresa Collins
             P.O. Box 392
             Chelsea, OK 74016

Tips for a Healthier-Happier You

• **Stop making excuses.** Don't wait for the perfect moment. By waiting you are putting your health and happiness on hold.

• **Believe in yourself.** Begin each morning by making a commitment to yourself. Remember to take it one meal at a time—one craving at a time—one day at a time.

• **Set short realistic goals.** Looking at the entire picture can be so overwhelming that it can hinder you from ever beginning. Reward yourself after a 5 to 10 pound loss with anything but food. Reaching your goals will become your springboard to total success.

• **Admire qualities in yourself right now.** Write down what you like about yourself; it could be your hair, eyes, etc. Post them where you can read them often. Loving yourself at this very moment will give you strength to begin and continue a healthier lifestyle.

• **Look your best every day.** The compliments you receive will be the boost you need to continue down that road of success.

• **Stop allowing food to be your source of happiness and best friend.** Food makes us feel good for a short while, but the guilt it leaves behind far outweighs the joy. Don't give in to that vicious cycle anymore.

• **Take your measurements.** What a motivator this can be. Write them down.

• **Take an honest look in the mirror.** • Accept the fact that your body is not perfect. • Know that you have the power to make changes in areas that you are not happy with. • Remember we are blessed with the fact that our bodies will shrink if we put out the effort.

• **Weekly weigh-ins are best.** Weigh in the morning, nude and on the same day of the week. Daily weigh-ins are misleading because our weight often fluctuates up or down. Write down your weekly weight.

7

- **Visualize yourself getting slimmer.** At least once per day close your eyes and visualize how good it feels not getting out of breath climbing stairs. Visualize how marvelous you look with your shirt tucked in those tiny jeans.

- **Exercise for life.** What you can live with is what you can stick with. Experiment with various exercises until you find one that suits your lifestyle. (Check with your doctor first before beginning any exercise program.)

- **Attitude is everything.** Go into changing your old habits slowly. Develop a sense of persistence and commitment to your new lifestyle.

- **Who are you losing weight for?** The answer must be for yourself. If you are losing weight for anyone else chances are you will harbor resentment and that could cost you your chance at success.

- **Practice portion control.** Meals or snack -- it does not matter -- this is a must. Just because a product says no fat, it does contain calories.

- **Learn to recognize when you are full.** Make a conscious effort to "feel" the full feeling in your stomach and when you do, STOP! It doesn't matter what is left on your plate, STOP!

- **Don't skip meals.** Eat a good breakfast; it will get your metabolism going. Skipping meals can cause you to overeat at some point in the day.

- **Drink at least 8 (8 ounce) glasses of water per day.** As far as I'm concerned water is the miracle drug. Water gives you a full feeling as well as keeping your body flushed out. I have found that if I drink water cold and through a straw I will consume it faster. It's also easier to make myself drink more.

- **Just aren't willing to give up some of your favorite foods?** That's OK. Find the no fat or low fat version, and go for it.

- **Be ready for the creeping Snack Attack.** When you bring home your snacks from the store or the ones you bake, divide

8

them into serving size portions and place them in sandwich bags. This will allow you to keep from overindulging when the snack attack hits.

• **Let yourself be human.** Realize that there will be times that we all allow ourselves to eat some of our favorite fattening foods. Compromise. Have one chocolate chip cookie versus three or four. Persistence is the key. Focus on your triumphs. After all, we are developing good habits that we can live with for life.

• **Make a conscious effort to do your grocery shopping on a full stomach.** Temptations are easier to resist if we are full. DO NOT SHOP AFTER WORK. Stress of the day could cause you to give in to temptation. When the products on the grocer's shelf are calling out your name, take control. Look at them and firmly say, "NO!"

• **Confide in someone you trust.** Make it someone who will listen to you, let you bare your soul about your challenging times, and share with you in your accomplishments.

The power lies within you to take control of your life. It's there, just let yourself reach for it. I'm not going to tell you that it won't be challenging at times... because it will. What I want you to do when those times creep in is stand in front of a mirror with your hand over your heart and look at yourself and say these words out loud: "I can – I will – I must do this for me. I am worth being healthy and I am worth being proud of me." The first few times I said those words to myself I cried. Over time they brought me strength. My greatest wish is that you will gain strength from them too.

You can bet that when you believe it in your heart first, the results you desire will follow a close second.

Love,
Teresa

Author's Notes

When following the recipes in this book, you will find that I have recommended the preferred products by name. I believe that these products give the best results.

Making "liquid" Butter Buds - Throughout this book I have used Butter Buds which come packaged in a box of eight individual envelopes. Following package directions when mixed with water, each envelope will make one-half cup of liquid butter substitute. This product can be found in the spice section of your grocery store, located near the other powdered forms of butter. Butter Buds can also be used dry and sprinkled over moist foods. I highly recommend this product. Butter Buds contain 5 calories per tablespoon of liquid and 0 grams of fat. All Natural Butter Buds Brand Butter Flavored Mix – 8 (1/2 oz.) packets.

Salt - Salt is always optional! It is not necessary to use salt in any of these recipes -- it is always offered as an optional seasoning.

Nuts - Nuts are always listed as optional! The quantity has been reduced in order to lower the amount of fat in the recipes. Toasting the nuts before adding them to the recipes will keep you from missing the quantity. Toasting nuts enhances their flavor. To toast nuts, place them in the broiler pan. Place the pan 3 inches from the flame. Toast for 2 minutes on the broil setting.

Non-stick Skillet - One of the best investments you will ever make for your low fat cooking is a good quality, large non stick skillet. It allows you to have great results without adding any fat!

Cooking Spray - This is a must! It comes in plain, butter, and olive oil flavors. Use in a non stick skillet for pan frying or coat cake pans in place of grease and flour. Also, spraying foods to be baked makes for a crispier coating.

Egg Substitute - Read labels carefully. Make sure the egg substitute you choose contains zero fat. My choice is Hiland egg substitute. You will find it located near the regular eggs in your supermarket.

Appetizers & Dips

"*Man often becomes what he believes himself to be. If I keep on saying to myself that I cannot do a certain thing, it is possible that I may end up by becoming incapable of doing it. On the contrary. If I have the belief that I can do it, I shall surely acquire the capacity to do it even if I may not have it at the beginning.*"

— Mahatma Gandhi

Fun Tips to Know

• Make going to the grocery store an adventure. You might as well have fun since you've got to be there anyway. Search out the new fat free and low fat products that are delivered to your grocer's shelves weekly. I have a major celebration in the aisle when I discover a new product that will bring happiness to my taste buds.

• Purchase as many reduced sodium products as you can. Also rinsing canned vegetables with water several times will remove even more sodium.

• For on the go muffins, simply place each cooled muffin on a sheet of wax paper. Bring up the sides and twist. Place individually wrapped muffins in a large zip lock bag. Freeze. When ready to use, peel off wax paper and heat in the microwave.

• Store coffee in the freezer. This will keep it fresher longer.

• Freeze left over coffee using ice cube trays. Place two cubes of frozen coffee and one cup fat free vanilla or chocolate ice cream in a blender or food processor. Blend until smooth. Yummy!

• Place sprigs of parsley in ice cube trays. Fill with water. Freeze. Store in freezer-safe zip lock bag. Thaw in water when ready to use.

• Place cut wedges of fruit in ice cube trays. Fill with water. Freeze. Store in freezer-safe zip lock bag. Makes for a pretty glass of tea or use in clear diet sodas.

Stuffed Cherry Tomatoes

Servings: 6   **Fat Grams: 0**

1/2 lb. cherry tomatoes
4 oz. nonfat cream cheese
1/4 pkg. Hidden Valley Ranch Salad Dressing Mix

Combine cream cheese and salad dressing mix. Stir well.
Core tomatoes. Stuff cheese mixture into tomatoes. Chill
well. Serve.

Pizza Fondue

Servings: Small Crowd   **Fat Grams: 4 in entire**
recipe

1 (32 oz.) jar zero fat spaghetti sauce
1 (8 oz.) pkg. Kraft fat free shredded Mozzarella cheese
1/4 c. Parmesan cheese
2 tsp. oregano
1 tsp. minced onion
1/4 tsp. garlic powder
2 loaves lowest fat garlic bread, cubed

Combine all ingredients except bread into microwave
safe bowl. Melt contents, stirring often. Pour into fondue
pot. Place garlic bread in serving bowl next to fondue pot
for easy dipping.

Cream Cheese Delights

Servings: Small Crowd   **Fat Grams: 10 in entire recipe**

1 (8 oz.) pkg. nonfat cream cheese, softened
1/2 c. nonfat sour cream
1 (4.25 oz.) can diced green chilies, drained
10 slices 98% fat free ham slices, sandwich cut
10 (8-inch) fat free flour tortillas
salsa

Combine cream cheese, sour cream, and green chilies in bowl. Blend well. Lay each tortilla on clean working area. Place 1 ham slice on each tortilla. Divide equally the cream cheese mixture onto each ham slice. Roll. Slice into 1/2 inch pieces. Arrange on serving tray. Cover and chill for 1 hour before serving. Serve a bowl of salsa with tray.

Bean Barrels
(Fun and Easy to Make)

Servings: 12   Fat Grams: Less than 1 per roll

1 pkg. corn tortillas
2 (16 oz.) fat free refried beans
2 T. green onions, chopped
1-1/2 cups Kraft fat free shredded cheddar cheese
toothpicks
1 (15 oz.) can fat free vegetarian chili

Preheat oven to 350 degrees. Coat cookie sheet with cooking spray. Heat tortillas in microwave for 40 seconds. Keep warm. Mix together beans, onions, and cheese. Add equal amounts of bean mixture to the heated tortillas. Roll. Secure with toothpick. Bake for 10 minutes in preheated oven or just until they start to brown. Dip each in hot chili.

Taco or Ranch Nibblers
"Delicious"

Servings: 6   **Fat Grams: 1.33 per serving**

1/2 c. water
2 T. liquid Butter Buds
1/2 envelope of either taco or Hidden Valley Ranch
        seasoning mix
2 whole chicken breasts, skinned, boned, and cut into
        1-inch pieces
toothpicks
nonfat sour cream

Heat in nonstick skillet water, butter buds, seasoning of choice. Stir. Add chicken pieces. Cook over medium heat for 10 minutes until chicken pieces are no longer pink. Drain, Arrange pieces on serving plate with bowl of nonfat sour cream in center. Serve with toothpicks. Dip and enjoy.

Bourbon Franks

Yields: 3 cups   **Fat Grams: 0 per serving/**
4 pieces

2 T. onion, chopped
1 T. liquid butter buds, + 2 T. water
1/2 c. catsup
1/3 c. brown sugar
3/4 c. bourbon
1 (14 oz.) pkg. Hormel fat free hot dogs

Sauté onion in liquid butter buds and water until tender. Drain. Over low heat add catsup, brown sugar, and bourbon to onions. Stir well. Cut each hot dog into four pieces and add to bourbon mixture. Simmer uncovered for 25 minutes. Serve hot.

Broiled Stuffed Mushrooms

Servings: 18   Fat Grams: 1.28 per stuffed
mushroom

18 med. mushrooms, cleaned
mushroom stems, chopped fine
3 T. liquid Butter Buds
5 strips turkey bacon cooked crisp and crumbled
1/3 c. grated Parmesan cheese

Place mushrooms, hollow-side up on broiler pan. Brush generously with liquid butter buds. Combine chopped stems, bacon and Parmesan cheese. Toss. Fill each mushroom with bacon mixture. Adjust broiler rack to 3-1/2 inches below heat source. Turn oven to 450 degrees. Broil for 7 to 8 minutes. Insert toothpicks into each one. Serve hot.

Cheese Zucchini Crisps

Servings: 4   **Fat Grams: 0**

1/3 c. corn flakes, crushed
2 T. Kraft Fat Free grated Parmesan cheese topping
1/2 tsp. seasoned salt
dash of garlic powder
4 small unpeeled zucchini, cut into thin 3-1/2-inch strips
1/4 c. liquid Butter Buds

Preheat oven to 375 degrees. Coat cookie sheet with vegetable spray. Mix together crumbs, Parmesan cheese, seasoned salt, and garlic powder. Dip zucchini into liquid butter buds, then toss into crumb mixture. Bake for 10 minutes or until crisp.

Small Tortilla Bowl

Servings: 1 per tortilla   **Fat Grams: 0**

6-inch fat free flour tortillas
warm water
10 oz. glass custard cups

Using warm water, brush tortillas with water to soften; do not saturate. Coat custard cup with cooking spray. Turn oven to 350 degrees. Press each tortilla into prepared custard cup. Bake for about 15 minutes or until lightly brown and crisp. Remove bowls from custard cups. Serve dips from them or use for salad bowls.

Baked Tortilla Chips
(Flour or Corn)

Servings: 12   **Fat Grams: 0 for flour**
                                                1 for corn

12 (6-inch) fat free flour tortillas
12 (6-inch) corn tortillas
Mrs. Dash's herb mixture
cinnamon sugar (only for flour tortillas)

Preheat oven to 350 degrees. Coat cookie sheet with butter flavor cooking spray. Using a pizza cutter, cut each tortilla as you would a pie with 8 triangles per tortilla. Lay each triangle onto a prepared cookie sheet. Coat each one with butter flavor cooking spray and sprinkle on your topping of choice. Bake in preheated oven for 5 minutes or just until crisp, not brown. Remove from cookie sheet and cool on wire rack. Store in airtight container.

Pineapple Cheese Ball

Servings: Small Crowd

Fat Grams: 0 Fat without pecans entire recipe 20.13 with pecans entire recipe

3 (8 oz.) pkg. nonfat cream cheese, softened
1 (6 oz.) can crushed pineapple, drained
1/4 c. pecans, chopped fine, optional

Mix cheese and pineapple. Form into large ball. Roll cheese ball in pecans. Place in center of serving platter. Cover and chill for 3 hours before serving. Serve with fruit wedges, vegetables, and low fat snack crackers.

Apple Dip

Yields: 1-3/4 cups

Fat Grams: 0

1 (8 oz.) pkg. nonfat cream cheese
1 (7 oz.) jar marshmallow cream
pinch of cinnamon
4 lg. assorted colors of apples,
    cut into wedges just before serving

Combine nonfat cream cheese and marshmallow cream in a bowl. Stir well. Pour into serving bowl. Sprinkle cinnamon on top. Chill for 1 hour before serving.

Waldorf Dip

Yields: 2 cups

Fat Grams: 5.03 for entire recipe; 0 without pecans

1 c. nonfat creamed cottage cheese
1/3 c. tart crisp apple, diced
1/4 c. celery, finely diced
1/2 tsp. lemon juice
1/2 tsp. sugar
2 T. pecans, chopped, optional

Combine cottage cheese, diced apple, diced celery, lemon juice and sugar in serving bowl. Stir lightly but thoroughly. Cover and chill for at least 2 hours before serving. Right before serving, sprinkle chopped pecans on top of dip. Great served with fruit and vegetable dippers.

Hot Cheese Dip

Servings: Small Crowd   Fat Grams: 0

1 lg. brick processed cheese (Healthy Choice),
   cut into large cubes
1 (14-1/2 oz.) can Mexican recipe stewed tomatoes
   (Del Monte)
1 (4.5 oz.) can green chilies, drained and diced

Place cheese cubes in microwave safe bowl. Melt, stirring frequently. Once cheese has melted, stir in tomatoes and green chilies. Serve with low fat tortilla style chips.

Bean Dip

Yields: 1-1/2 cups   Fat Grams: 0 in entire dip

1 (16 oz.) can fat free refried beans
1/4 c. diced tomatoes and green chilies
1/4 c. Kraft fat free shredded Cheddar cheese
garlic salt to taste

Combine all ingredients in microwave safe bowl. Stir well. Heat in microwave until thoroughly heated. Serve with low fat tortilla style chips and nonfat sour cream.

Guilt Free Guacamole

Yields: 2 cups   **Fat Grams: 0 in entire recipe**

1 (10 oz.) pkg. frozen peas, thawed
1/8 c. lemon juice or lime juice
1/2 envelope taco seasoning (more to taste)
1/2 c. Kraft fat free Miracle Whip salad dressing
1/4 c. picante sauce or salsa
3 T. onion, chopped
1 small tomato, chopped

Combine in food processor or blender, the peas, lemon juice, taco seasoning, and salad dressing. Blend until smooth. Pour into serving bowl. Stir in picante sauce, onion, and tomato and mix until well blended. (Reserve a small amount of tomato for garnish in center of dip.) Chill for 1 hour to allow flavors to blend. Serve with fat free or low fat tortilla chips.

Guacamole Dip

Yields: 2 cups

Fat Grams: 3.75
1/4 c. serving

1 med. ripe avocado
1/2 c. Kraft fat free Miracle Whip salad dressing
2 T. lemon juice (prevents avocado from turning brown)
salt to taste, optional
1 tsp. grated onion
1/4 tsp. liquid hot sauce
1 lg. tomato, peeled and chopped
nonfat sour cream

Peel, remove pit, and mash avocado. Add remaining ingredients and stir well. Cover and chill for 30 minutes before serving. Great served with low fat tortilla style chips and topped with nonfat sour cream.

Zesty Dip

Yields: 2 cups   **Fat Grams: 2 in entire recipe**

1 (3 oz.) pkg. nonfat cream cheese
1 c. nonfat sour cream
2 tsp. lemon juice
1 envelope Italian salad dressing mix
1/2 c. finely chopped, cooked shrimp or canned shrimp,
    drained

Combine all ingredients in a bowl. Stir to mix well. Chill for at least 3 hours before serving. Great served with vegetables or low fat crackers.

Spinach Dip
(A Personal Favorite)

Yields: 2 cups   **Fat Grams: 0 in entire dip**

1 (10 oz.) pkg. frozen chopped spinach, thawed and
    squeezed dry
1 green onion, chopped fine
1 (8 oz.) can water chestnuts, drained and chopped
1 c. nonfat sour cream
1/2 c. Kraft fat free Miracle Whip salad dressing
1 (8 oz.) envelope vegetable soup mix

Combine all ingredients into bowl. Stir well. Pour into serving bowl. Cover and chill for 1 hour before serving. Serve with assorted vegetables or low fat snack crackers.

Clam-Cheese Dip

Yields: 1-1/3 cups   Fat Grams: 1.55 for entire recipe

1 med. clove garlic
1 (8-1/2 oz.) can minced clams, drain and reserve
    1 T. liquid
1 (6 oz.) pkg. nonfat cream cheese
1 tsp. Worcestershire sauce
1 tsp. lemon juice
1/2 tsp. salt, optional

Rub the inside of a serving bowl well with the cut end of garlic. Set bowl aside. Chop clams fine. Add 1 T. of clam juice, nonfat cream cheese, Worcestershire sauce, lemon juice, and salt. Blend ingredients thoroughly. Pour into serving bowl. Cover and chill at least 3 hours before serving. Serve with low fat crackers or great stuffed in celery sticks.

Get Excited About Steamed Fruits & Vegetables
(My kids love the taste of steamed vegetables)

My electric steamer is an inexpensive easy to use tool that is used almost daily in my kitchen. By steaming our fruits and vegetables I know that I have helped our food retain their precious vitamins and minerals that are essential to our good health. Once you taste steamed vegetables for yourself you may never again place them in a pot of boiling water!

Listed below are some of my family's favorites:

- Apples - Raisins - Carrots (sliced thin)
- Apples cored - cinnamon, brown sugar, oatmeal, (stuff in cored apple)
- Broccoli - Yellow onion slices
- Brussel Sprouts - (add a capful of lemon juice to water)
- Cabbage - Sliced Red Apple rings
- Carrots - Cauliflower
- Corn On The Cob - Mint leaves added to water (2)
- Red Potatoes (leave skin on) - Whole green beans
- Squash - Yellow Crook Neck or Zucchini (sliced in strips) - Yellow Onion Slices - sprinkle 1 tsp. of bacon bits over squash

Note: In place of water, substitute fat free chicken broth. Try adding lemon juice and orange juice to the water. Don't forget to use I Can't Believe It's Not Butter Spray for a melt in your mouth taste.

Soups, Salads & Sandwiches

"A strong positive mental attitude will create more miracles than any wonder drug."

— **Patricia Neal**

Write to Lose

• Keep a journal of true feelings. Be honest with yourself. But, more important, write about your accomplishments. Read them often. This allows you to see not only how far your body has come, but more important, how far *you* have come!

• Create an inspirational scrapbook. This is a fun way to keep you motivated. Place a before photo in it and follow up with monthly ones. As you shrink into smaller clothes, keep the tags and write the dates on them. Place other people's success stories that you've clipped out of magazines in your book. Read them often. Picture the day you write your own success story. Add other magazine articles that will benefit your efforts—such as helpful tips, etc. Anything you can think of that will get you motivated and keep you motivated is important.

• Surround your home, car, and workplace with motivational sayings or quotes. Read them often and out loud. These serve as wonderful pep talks to ourselves.

"You must do the thing you think you cannot do."
Eleanor Roosevelt

Chicken Salad
(Always a hit at family get-togethers!)

Servings: 8 **Fat Grams: 2.6 per serving with pecans**

1-1/4 lb. chicken breasts, skinned, cooked,
    cut into 1/2-inch pieces
1 c. celery, thinly sliced
1 c. red or green seedless grapes, cut into halves
1/2 c. seedless raisins
1/2 c. pineapple nonfat yogurt
1/4 c. Kraft fat free Miracle Whip salad dressing
1/4 c. pineapple chunks, drained well
2 T. onion, chopped fine
1 tsp. dried tarragon leaves
1/2 tsp. salt, optional
1/8 tsp. ground white pepper
2 T. chopped pecans, optional
lettuce leaves for garnish

Combine all ingredients in bowl. Stir well. Chill for 1 hour. Line edges of bowl with lettuce leaves, place chicken salad in bowl. Serve.

Suggestion: This chicken salad is wonderful served in whole wheat pita pocket halves. Use fat free pita bread.

Chicken Caesar Salad

Servings: 4   Fat Grams: 5.5 per serving

4 chicken breasts, boned, skinned, cut into thin strips
5 c. romaine lettuce, torn into bite-size pieces
1 lg. red tomato, diced
1 sm. red onion, halved, sliced thin
1 oz. cubed Feta cheese, crumbled
fat free Caesar or Italian dressing
fat free croutons

Brown chicken with cooking spray in non-stick skillet. Cook until no longer pink in the center. Toss together lettuce, tomato, onion, and chicken strips. Sprinkle feta cheese on top. Serve with choice of fat free croutons and nonfat salad dressing.

Taco Salad
(Always a Hit!)

Servings: 4   **Fat Grams: 1**

1 lb. ground turkey breast
1 envelope taco seasoning
1 lg. tomato, diced
1 lg. head lettuce, shredded
1 med. onion, diced
1 (15 oz.) can kidney beans, drained and rinsed
1-1/2 c. Kraft fat free shredded cheddar cheese
1/4 c. green bell pepper, diced
nonfat or low fat tortilla chips
1 (8 oz.) bottle fat free Catalina dressing

Cook ground turkey with taco seasoning. Add 1/4 c. of water to turkey mixture while cooking. Drain. Toss all ingredients together. Serve on a bed of nonfat or low fat tortilla chips or follow directions for small tortilla bowls in the appetizer section of this book.

Alternate version: omit dressing and serve on a bed of chips, topped with salsa and sour cream. Either way, it's a hit!

Zero Fat Potato Salad

Servings: 6   **Fat Grams: 0**

2 c. cooked potatoes, diced
2 boiled eggs; remove the yolks and chop the whites
1 sm. onion, chopped
1/3 c. dill pickles, chopped
1 t. celery seed
1 T. vinegar
1 tsp. sugar
salt and pepper to taste
1/4 c. Kraft fat free Miracle Whip salad dressing
parsley flakes or paprika for garnish

Combine all ingredients in a large bowl, tossing lightly to mix. Place in serving bowl and garnish with parsley flakes or paprika. Cover and chill for 2 hours to blend flavors.

Creamy Macaroni Salad
(Just like at restaurant buffets without all the fat!)

Servings: 8   Fat Grams: 0.5

1 (16 oz.) pkg. macaroni, cooked, drained, cooled
1 lg. green bell pepper, seeded, chopped
3 carrots, peeled and grated
1 sm. onion, chopped

Dressing:
1 c. white vinegar
3/4 c. sugar
2 c. Kraft fat free Miracle Whip salad dressing
1 (14 oz.) can fat free sweetened, condensed milk
pinch of salt (optional)

Combine cooled macaroni, bell pepper, carrots, and onion in a large serving bowl. Stir together vinegar, sugar, salad dressing, milk, and salt. Pour dressing over macaroni mixture. Toss well to coat. Cover and chill for at least 6 hours or overnight before serving.

Macaroni Salad

Servings: 4 **Fat Grams: .25**

1 c. Rotini, plain, or garden variety corkscrew-type macaroni
2 sm. carrots, peeled or julienned
2 green onions, chopped with tops
1 (2 oz.) jar diced pimientos, drained
3/4 c. diced celery
1/4 c. frozen peas, thawed
2 T. parsley, chopped
10 cherry tomatoes, halved
1/4 c. fat free Italian salad dressing
2 T. Kraft fat free Miracle Whip salad dressing
1/8 tsp. pepper
Lettuce leaves for garnish

Cook macaroni according to package directions, omitting salt and oil. Drain. Rinse with cool water. Combine in large bowl, carrots, onions, pimientos, celery, peas, and parsley. Add macaroni. Toss well Mix fat free Italian salad dressing, fat free Miracle Whip, and pepper. Stir well. Pour over salad. Stir lightly to coat. Chill for 2 hours before serving. Arrange lettuce leaves around sides of serving platter. Place salad on serving platter and serve.

Sweet Fruit Slaw

Servings: 10   **Fat Grams: 0**

1 med. head cabbage, shredded
1 med. apple, diced
1 (11 oz.) can mandarin oranges, drained
1/2 c. white seedless grapes, halved
1/4 c. raisins
1 c. fat free Miracle Whip salad dressing
1/4 c. sugar
2 T. white vinegar
1 T. prepared mustard
1/2 tsp. celery seed

Combine cabbage, apple, mandarin oranges, grapes, and raisins. Toss. Place salad dressing, sugar, vinegar, mustard, and celery seed in a shaker. Shake well and pour dressing over slaw. Toss well. Cover and chill for 1 hour before serving. Toss lightly before serving.

Cranberry Salad

Servings: 8–10

Fat Grams: 0
2.01 with pecans

2 c. cranberries, ground (1 lb. raw)
1 c. sugar
1 (3 oz.) pkg. raspberry gelatin
1 (6 oz.) can crushed pineapple, drained
1 (11 oz.) can mandarin oranges, drained
1 lg. red apple (not peeled), grated
1/4 c. pecans, chopped, optional
1 (16 oz.) pkg. miniature marshmallows

Combine sugar and cranberries in large bowl. Let stand until sugar dissolves. Prepare gelatin following package directions. Let cool. Mix gelatin with the cranberry mixture, crushed pineapple, mandarin oranges, grated apple and pecans. Stir well. Place in pretty serving bowl, cover, and chill overnight or 6 hours. Just before serving sprinkle marshmallows on top.

I dedicate this to my mom. Mom's Thanksgiving table would not be complete without the pretty red dish filled with her cranberry salad.

Onion-Orange Tossed Salad

Servings: 4   **Fat Grams: 0**

1 sm. head iceberg lettuce, coarsely shredded
1 sm. red onion, cut in thinly sliced rings
1 (6 oz.) can mandarin oranges, drained
1/4 c. Zesty Italian fat free salad dressing
sugar to taste
pinch crushed red pepper

Combine lettuce, onion, and oranges in salad bowl. Toss. Mix separately the salad dressing, sugar, and red pepper. Pour salad dressing mixture over tossed salad. Toss. Chill for 30 minutes before serving. Toss before serving.

Pretty Tomato Salad

Servings: 8   **Fat Grams: 3.45**

18 red cherry tomatoes, cut in halves
18 small yellow pear tomatoes, cut lengthwise in halves
8 plum tomatoes, cut lengthwise in quarters
1 lg. yellow tomato, cut crosswise in 1/2-inch slices
1 lg. red tomato cut crosswise in 1/2-inch slices
3/4 c. white wine vinegar
1/8 tsp. salt, optional
1/8 tsp. ground white pepper
2 T. olive oil
1-1/2 T. lemon juice
2 T. chopped chives, fresh or 1 T. dried
1/4 c. shallots
2 T. black olives, chopped

Place vinegar and salt in a shaker and shake until salt dissolves. Add pepper, lemon juice, chives, shallots, olives, and olive oil to shaker. Shake lightly to blend oil with vinegar. Pour marinade and toss tomatoes lightly to coat. Cover and place in a cool location, but not in refrigerator. Let stand for 2 hours before serving. Toss lightly just before serving.

Suggestion: Save any left over marinade and use it to coat any raw vegetables or for a marinade in pita pocket sandwiches. Store left over marinade in refrigerator.

Three Bean Salad

Servings: 6   **Fat Grams: 0**

2 (15 oz.) can three bean salad (Green Giant)
2 T. fat free Zesty Italian salad dressing
sugar to taste

Combine all ingredients in serving bowl. Toss well. Chill for 2 hours before serving. Toss just before serving.

Mandarin Orange Salad

Servings: 6   **Fat Grams: 0**

1 (8 oz.) carton nonfat cottage cheese
2 (3 oz.) pkg. orange gelatin
1 (6 oz.) can crushed pineapple, well drained
1 (6 oz.) can mandarin oranges, drained
1 (9 oz.) carton nonfat Cool Whip

Combine cottage cheese and powdered gelatin. Stir well. Add to gelatin mixture crushed pineapple and mandarin oranges. Stir well. Fold in nonfat Cool Whip. Chill for 2 hours before serving.

Fat Free Watergate Salad

Servings: 6 **Fat Grams: 0**
3.35 with pecans

1 (9 oz.) Cool Whip
1 (3.4 oz.) fat free pistachio instant pudding
1 (20 oz.) can crushed pineapple, drained
1 c. miniature marshmallows
1/4 c. pecans, chopped, optional

Combine Cool Whip and pudding. Fold in crushed pineapple, marshmallows and pecans. Chill for 2 hours before serving.

Zero Fat Creamy Garlic Dressing

Yields: 3-1/2 cups   **Fat Grams: 0**

2 c. Kraft fat free Miracle Whip salad dressing
1/2 c. water
3 cloves garlic, minced
1 T. white vinegar
1/2 c. fat free half-and-half (Land O' Lakes)
2 T. garlic powder
1/2 T. prepared mustard

Combine all ingredients in a blender or food processor. Place on low setting and blend for 2 minutes. Store in airtight container in refrigerator. Will keep for several days.

Mock Sour Cream

Yields: 20 tablespoons   **Fat Grams: 0**

3 T. lemon juice
1 tsp. salt, optional
1/4 tsp. prepared mustard
1 c. plain nonfat yogurt

Mix lemon juice and salt. Stir until salt dissolves. Blend mustard into lemon juice mixture. Stir mustard mixture into yogurt slowly. Mix well. Chill for 1 hour before serving.

Papa Don's Chili

Servings: 6   **Fat Grams: .67**

1 lb. extra lean ground turkey breast
2 cloves garlic, minced
1 green bell pepper, seeded, chopped
1 red bell pepper, seeded, chopped
2 c. fresh mushrooms, sliced
1/2 c. onion, chopped
1 (32 oz.) can diced tomatoes
1 (14.5 oz.) can stewed tomatoes
1 (15 oz.) can tomato sauce
1 (15 oz.) can chili beans, mild or hot
2 c. sliced zucchini
1-1/4 c. frozen corn
1 envelope chili seasoning
1/2 c. dark brown sugar
1-1/2 c. Kraft fat free shredded cheddar cheese

Cook ground turkey in 1/4 c. water. Use a potato masher when cooking ground turkey to keep the meat from clumping. Drain. Rinse meat using a colander to remove excess fat. Combine in soup pot cooked turkey, garlic, bell peppers, mushrooms, onions, diced tomatoes, stewed tomatoes, tomato sauce, chili beans, zucchini, corn, chili seasoning, and brown sugar. Cook over medium heat for 30 minutes. Reduce heat and simmer over low for 1 hour. If needed, add 1/4 cup of water to obtain desired consistency. Serve in individual bowls and garnish with nonfat cheese.

I dedicate this to my dad, otherwise known by his 6 grandkids as Papa Don. When visiting Grandpa's house we always look forward to either a hearty bowl of soup or a spicy bowl of chili.

Working Mom's Chili

Servings: 4   Fat Grams: 2

2 lbs. ground turkey breast
1 c. celery, chopped
1 (14-1/2 oz.) can tomato juice
1 (14-1/2 oz.) can fat free chili beans
1 med. onion, chopped
1 (14-1/2 oz.) can whole tomatoes (slightly mashed)
chili powder to taste
1 (14-1/2 oz.) can pork and beans
brown sugar to taste

Brown ground turkey with 1/4 cup water. Drain. Stir in all ingredients. Simmer until bubbly hot. Enjoy.

Chicken Soup

Servings: 4   **Fat Grams: 2.5**

1 whole chicken breast, skinned and halved
3/4 c. water
1/4 c. onion, chopped
1/4 c. carrot, chopped
1/4 c. celery, chopped
1 (10-1/2 oz.) can Campbell's Healthy Request Chicken
      Soup
3/4 c. skim milk
1/2 c. Kraft fat free shredded Cheddar cheese

Combine chicken, water, onion, carrot, and celery in saucepan. Cover and cook until chicken and vegetables are tender. Remove chicken and shred. Return chicken to saucepan. Add soup and milk. Stir. Cook until soup becomes bubbly hot. Remove from heat. Stir in cheese until thoroughly melted.

New England Style Clam Chowder

Servings: 6 **Fat Grams: 3.88**

1 (7-1/2 oz.) can minced clams, drain and reserve broth
1/4 c. turkey bacon, cooked crisp, crumbled
1/4 c. onion, chopped
1 c. potatoes, peeled, diced
1/2 tsp. salt, optional
dash of pepper
2 c. skim milk
1 T. parsley, chopped

Add enough water to reserved clam liquid to equal 1 cup. Add 1/4 cup of water to Dutch oven. Add onions. Cook until onions become tender and transparent. Add clam liquid, diced potatoes, salt, and pepper. Cover and cook for 15 minutes or until potatoes are tender. Add skim milk and clams. Heat thoroughly. Garnish with parsley.

Potato Soup

Servings: 4   **Fat Grams: 0**

3 c. potatoes, peeled and cubed
1/4 c. onion, chopped fine
2 T. all-purpose flour
2 c. skim milk
1/4 c. liquid Butter Buds
parsley flakes for garnish

Combine potatoes and onions in soup pot. Fill with just enough water to cover potatoes. Cook until potatoes are tender. Drain. Blend flour with 1/2 cup of milk to form a smooth thickening. Set aside. Stir remaining milk into soup pot. Cook over medium heat until bubbly. Add flour mixture to thicken. Cook for 1 minute longer. Garnish with parsley.

According to my mom and grandma one of the first words I learned to speak was "soup." I might have known one of my first words would have been about food.

White Bean Soup

Servings: 4   Fat Grams: 1.6

1 (16 oz.) can navy beans, undrained
1 (15.8 oz.) can great northern beans, undrained
1 c. water
1/4 c. onion, chopped
1 carrot, peeled and diced
1/4 c. liquid Butter Buds
1 c. fully cooked 98% fat free ham, cubed
parsley flakes

Combine navy beans and great northern beans in a large saucepan. Mash slightly using potato masher. Stir in water. Cook over low heat for 8 minutes or until thoroughly heated. Meanwhile sauté onion and carrots in non-stick skillet using butter spray and 1/4 cup water. Cook until carrots and onions become tender. Drain. Add sautéed mixture to beans. Stir in liquid butter buds and ham. Cook over low heat for 10 minutes. Stir occasionally. Garnish with parsley flakes.

Okra and Tomato Soup

Servings: 6   **Fat Grams: 0**

4 c. okra, sliced
4 lg. tomatoes, peeled and chopped
1 med. onion, diced
1/2 tsp. white vinegar (removes slime from okra)
salt and pepper to taste, optional

Combine all ingredients in a large saucepan. Cover with water and cook over medium heat until okra is tender. Salt and pepper to taste.

Broccoli Cheese Soup

Servings: 4   **Fat Grams: 0**

1 small head of broccoli, diced
1 med. yellow onion, diced
1 tsp. celery flakes
salt and pepper to taste, optional
2 tsp. chicken soup base
3 T. flour
8 c. skim milk
1/2 brick Healthy Choice process cheese, cubed

Combine broccoli, onions, celery flakes, salt, pepper, and chicken soup base in a large saucepan. Add enough water to cover broccoli. Cook over high heat for 12 minutes or until onions and broccoli become crisp tender. Drain. Mix flour and small amount of skim milk to form thickening. Pour over vegetables. Add rest of skim milk and cubed cheese. Cook over low heat. Stir to melt cheese. Serve immediately.

Egg Drop Soup

Servings: 4   **Fat Grams: 0**

2 (10-3/4 oz.) cans fat free chicken broth
4 c. water
1/2 c. egg substitute
2 T. liquid Butter Buds
cornstarch for thickening
2 T. parsley flakes
pepper to taste

Bring chicken broth and water to boil in a large saucepan. Whisk slowly one-half of the egg substitute into boiling chicken mixture. Repeat process with remaining egg substitute. Thicken with cornstarch. Add parsley flakes and pepper. Stir. Serve hot.

Split Pea Soup

Servings: 6   **Fat Grams: 1.13**

1 c. split green peas
5 c. water
1 c. 98% fat free ham, diced
1 onion diced
bay leaf
2 T. liquid Butter Buds
1 T. parsley, chopped

Place peas in bowl. Cover with water and soak overnight. Drain. Combine peas, 5 cups water, ham, onion, bay leaf, and liquid butter buds in large saucepan. Cover and cook over low heat for 3 hours. Remove bay leaf. Garnish with chopped parsley.

Zesty Chicken Sandwich

Servings: 4   **Fat Grams: 4**

4 boneless chicken breasts, skinned
1/2 c. fat free Zesty Italian salad dressing
4 hamburger buns
1 c. Kraft fat free shredded cheddar cheese
fat free Miracle Whip salad dressing

Dip each breast in salad dressing. Lay each breast on broiler rack. Broil for 2 minutes. Turn and baste with dressing. Broil for another 2 minutes. Repeat process until chicken is fully cooked. Place broiled chicken on bottom half of each bun. Add equal amounts of cheese on top of each chicken breast. Brush top bun with fat free Miracle Whip. Heat in microwave for 30 seconds to melt cheese.

Chicken-Cheese Sandwich

Servings: 4   Fat Grams: 4

4 skinless, boneless chicken breasts
butter flavor cooking spray
4 hamburger buns
4 fat free cheese slices, American or Mozzarella
Kraft fat free Miracle Whip salad dressing

Coat non-stick skillet with butter flavored cooking spray. Place chicken in prepared non-stick skillet. Brown on both sides until fully cooked and no longer pink in the center. Lay each chicken breast on bottom half of hamburger bun. Place cheese on top. Spread salad dressing on top bun. Put together. Serve with salad. What a meal! Enjoy!

Chicken Turnovers

Servings: 6   **Fat Grams: 2**

1/2 c. green bell pepper
1/4 c. onion, chopped
1/4 c. water
2 T. liquid Butter Buds
2 c. chicken breasts, skinned, cooked, chopped
1 (8 oz.) can applesauce
1/2 tsp. ground ginger
salt to taste, optional
2 pkg. refrigerated biscuits (1.5 fat grams for 2 biscuits)
skim milk
sesame seed

Combine in large non-stick skillet bell pepper, onion, water and liquid butter buds. Sauté until onion becomes tender. Remove from heat. Add to skillet mixture chicken, applesauce, mustard, ginger, and salt. On lightly floured surface roll each biscuit to form a 5-inch circle. Place 1/3 cup of chicken mixture on 6 dough circles. Spread mixture to within 1/2 inch from edge. Place remaining dough circles over top of chicken mixture. Moisten fork with skim milk and seal edges. Brush dough with remaining milk and sprinkle sesame seeds on top. Bake in prepared pan in a preheated oven for 10 to 12 minutes or until golden brown.

Ham Roll-Ups

Servings: 4   **Fat Grams: 2**

1/4 c. cucumber, chopped
1/4 c. tomato, chopped
1/4 c. fresh mushrooms, sliced
2 T. ripe, pitted olives, sliced
2 T. green onion, sliced
1/3 c. fat free Zesty Italian salad dressing
1 (6 oz.) pkg. sliced ham (1 fat gram per slice)
1 c. Kraft fat free shredded Mozzarella cheese
4 large lettuce leaves
4 toothpicks

Combine cucumber, tomato, mushrooms, olives, green onions, and Italian dressing. Toss. Cover and chill for 6 hours or overnight. Drain well. Spread out on clean surface, each lettuce leaf. Place 2 ham slices in center of each lettuce leaf. Next place 1/4 cup of vegetable mixture and 1/4 cup fat free Mozzarella cheese. Roll up each one and fasten with toothpicks.

Vegetables

"What small potatoes we all are compared with what we might be!"

— **Charles Dudley Warner**

Spice Up Your Life

One of the keys to successful weight loss is a feeling of being satisfied. Spices can do this. They also help reduce the urge to load vegetables with butter and margarines. These are just a few suggestions. Have fun coming up with your own combinations. Remember to buy spices and herbs in small quantities and store them away from the heat.

Vegetable	Spice or Herb
Asparagus	sesame seed, tarragon
Beans	cumin, nutmeg, thyme, mint
Broccoli	nutmeg
Brussel sprouts	nutmeg
Cabbage	caraway, dill
Carrots	cinnamon, cloves, nutmeg, dill
Cauliflower	nutmeg
Corn	mint, red pepper
Mushrooms	oregano, rosemary, tarragon
Peas	mint, parsley
Potatoes	dill, rosemary, basil, chives, mint
Salad Greens	chives, tarragon
Spinach	nutmeg
Squash	oregano, allspice, cloves, cinnamon, parsley
Tomatoes	basil, dill, oregano

"Rich" Potato Bake

Servings: 6   **Fat Grams: 0**

**1 (32 oz.) bag of frozen Ore Ida fat free hash browns
(southern style potatoes, thawed)
3 c. Land O' Lakes fat free half and half
1/4 c. liquid Butter Buds
1 (16 oz.) pkg. Kraft fat free shredded cheddar cheese**

Preheat oven to 350 degrees. Coat a 9 x 13 x 2 baking pan with cooking spray. Place hash browns in bottom of baking pan; spread out evenly. Combine half and half and Butter Buds in small bowl and stir. Pour the half and half mixture over the potatoes. Sprinkle pepper according to taste. Spread the cheese over the top of potatoes. Bake for 1 hour. Let stand a few minutes before serving.

Tangy Potatoes

Servings: 8   **Fat Grams: 0**

1 c. nonfat sour cream
1/2 c. skim milk
1 T. onion, minced
5 c. peeled and diced cooked potatoes
salt and pepper to taste, optional
2 T. fine dry bread crumbs
(1 gram of fat or less per serving)
1 T. liquid Butter Buds

Preheat oven to 350 degrees. Coat a large casserole dish with cooking spray. Combine in a medium mixing bowl nonfat sour cream, skim milk, and onion. Mix well. Place half of the diced potatoes into the bottom of casserole. Pour half of the sour cream mixture over the top of potatoes. Sprinkle salt and pepper over sour cream mixture. Repeat above process with the remaining ingredients. In a small bowl mix together bread crumbs and Butter Buds. Sprinkle bread crumb mixture on top of last layer. Bake for 20 to 25 minutes.

Cheese'n Potato Wafers

Servings: 6   **Fat Grams: 0**

4 lg. potatoes, unpeeled thinly sliced
1/4 c. liquid Butter Buds
1 T. onion, minced
salt and pepper to taste, optional
1-1/2 c. Kraft fat free shredded Cheddar cheese
1 T. parsley flakes

Preheat oven to 425 degrees. Coat a 13 x 9 x 2 baking dish with cooking spray. Combine in small bowl butter buds, onion, salt, and pepper. Layer potato slices in prepared dish. Pour over top of potato slices Butter Bud mixture; toss lightly to coat. Bake uncovered for 45 minutes or until potatoes are tender. Remove from oven. Sprinkle cheese and parsley on top. Return to oven just until cheese melts.

Potato Wedges

Servings: 4   **Fat Grams: 0**

4 med. russet potatoes with skin, cut into wedges
butter flavor cooking spray
season salt or Mrs. Dash

Preheat oven to 400 degrees. Lightly coat baking sheet with cooking spray. Spread wedges evenly on baking sheet. Spray wedges with butter flavor cooking spray. Bake for 45 minutes or until tender and golden brown. Sprinkle with season salt or Mrs. Dash.

Zesty Potato Wedges

Servings: 4   **Fat Grams: Trace**

4 med. russet potatoes with skins, cut into wedges
2 T. light Italian dressing

Preheat oven to 400 degrees. Coat baking sheet with cooking spray. Combine potato wedges and light dressing in large bowl. Toss. Place wedges individually on prepared sheet. Bake for 45 minutes or until potatoes are tender and golden brown.

Note: You may baste potato wedges with remaining dressing during baking period.

Provincial AuGratin Potatoes

Servings: 6   Fat Grams: 2.33

1 (10) oz. pkg. augratin potato mix
1 c. dry white wine or cooking white wine
1 T. olive oil
1 tsp. garlic, minced
1/4 c. parsley, chopped
1/2 c. tomato, chopped
1/2 c. lemon juice

Follow package directions, but substitute white wine for 1 cup water. Stir in remaining ingredients. Bake in oven or microwave.

Oven Fried Vegetables
(Okra or Squash or Onion Rings)

Servings: 4   **Fat Grams: 0**

Coating Mixture
1-1/2 c. Kellogg's Corn Flake Crumbs
salt and pepper to taste, optional
Mrs. Dash

Coat jelly roll pan with butter flavor cooking spray. Bake in preheated oven at 350 degrees for 25 to 30 minutes. Variations: Okra (Use 16 ounce package of frozen okra, thawed. Place okra and crumbs in bowl with lid. Shake. Spray with butter flavor cooking spray.) Squash (Use 1 medium yellow or zucchini squash, sliced, 1/2 cup skim milk. Soak squash in milk. Drain. Repeat coating and spraying process as with okra.) Onion (Use 1 large onion, sliced and separated. Follow the directions above for squash.)

Baked Vegetables
"Mouthwatering"

Servings: 6   **Fat Grams: 0**

2 lg. stalks celery, cut into 8 pieces
6 med. carrots, peeled, halved
2 lg. onions, cut in half
6 potatoes, peeled, cut in half
1/2 sm. head cabbage, cut into 4 slices
1 (15 oz.) can cut green beans
1 (14-1/2 oz.) can fat free chicken broth
1/4 c. liquid Butter Buds

Preheat oven to 350 degrees. Coat baking pan with cooking spray. Arrange all vegetables in prepared pan. Pour over vegetables chicken broth and butter bud mixture. Sprinkle with pepper. Cover lightly with foil. Bake for 1 hour or until all vegetables are tender.

Raisin Baked Beans
"Wonderful Side Dish"

Yields: 1 quart   Fat Grams: 1.6 per serving

1/2 c. seedless raisins
1 sm. onion chopped
1 tart apple, peeled and chopped
1/2 c. extra lean, fully cooked ham, cubed
1 (1 lb., 15 oz.) can fat free baked beans (Bush's)
1-1/2 tsp. dry mustard
1/4 c. sweet pickle relish
1/2 c. catsup

Preheat oven to 300 degrees. Place all ingredients in a large bean pot or casserole. Stir. Bake for 2 hours.

Green Bean Casserole

Servings: 6   Fat Grams: 1.17

1 (14-1/2 oz.) can French cut green beans
1 (10-3/4 oz.) can Campbell's Healthy Request
        cream of chicken soup
1/2 c. Kraft fat free shredded Cheddar cheese
1/4 c. fat free bread crumbs
1 T. liquid Butter Buds
2 T. onion, chopped

Preheat oven to 325 degrees. Coat a 1-1/2 quart casserole with cooking spray. Alternate layers of beans, soup, and cheese. Mix together bread crumbs, Butter Buds, and onions. Sprinkle bread crumb mixture on top and bake in preheated oven for 1 hour.

French Peas

Servings: 4   Fat Grams 2.5

4 slices turkey bacon, cooked, crumbled
    (2.5 fat grams per 2 slices)
1/2 c. Land O' Lakes fat free half and half
1/2 tsp. all-purpose flour
1 (14-1/2 oz.) can peas, drained
1 (6 oz.) can sliced mushrooms, drained

Combine in saucepan half-and-half and bring to a boil. Thicken by adding small amounts of flour at a time. Remove pan from heat. Stir in peas and mushrooms. Return to low heat to warm peas and mushrooms. Stir in crumbled bacon just before serving.

Creamed Broccoli

Servings: 4   Fat Grams: 1.25

1 (10 oz.) pkg. frozen broccoli
1/2 c. Healthy Choice process cheese, cubed
1 (10 -3/4 oz.) can Campbell's Healthy Request
    cream of mushroom soup

Preheat oven to 350 degrees. Coat a 1 quart casserole with cooking spray. Place frozen broccoli in prepared casserole. Add cheese; spoon on soup. Cover and bake in preheated oven for 1 hour.

Asparagus with Hollandaise Sauce

Servings: 4   Fat Grams: 1.5

1 (10-3/4 oz.) can Campbell's Healthy Request
     cream of mushroom soup
2 T. lemon juice
1/4 c. Kraft fat free Miracle Whip salad dressing
1 (14 oz.) can asparagus spears, drained

(Tip: Be sure to open the can of asparagus from the bottom to keep the tips from breaking!)

Heat soup, lemon juice, and salad dressing in saucepan. Do not boil. Arrange drained asparagus on serving dish. Pour sauce over them. Serve immediately.

Corn and Cheese Bake

Servings: 6   **Fat Grams: 0**

4 c. canned whole kernel corn, drained
2 T. flour
1/2 c. egg substitute
2 T. sugar
1/2 c. skim milk
1/4 lb. Healthy choice fat free process cheese

Preheat oven to 350 degrees. Coat a 2-quart casserole with cooking spray. Combine corn, flour, egg substitute, sugar, and skim milk. Cut the fat free cheese into chunks. Stir to mix well. Pour into prepared casserole. Cover tightly with foil and bake for 30 to 40 minutes.

Yellow Squash and Stewed Tomatoes

Servings: 4   Fat Grams: Less than 1

**2 slices turkey bacon cooked crisp and crumbled
    (2.5 fat grams per 2 slices)
1/2 c. water
1 T. liquid Butter Buds
1 med. yellow squash, sliced paper thin
1/2 med. onion, sliced thin
1 (14-1/2 oz.) can stewed tomatoes
1 (6 oz.) can tomato sauce
1/2 tsp. dried sweet basil
1 T. Kraft fat free grated Parmesan cheese topping**

In a large saucepan add water, Butter buds, squash, and onions. Cook until vegetables are tender. Do not drain. Add stewed tomatoes and tomato sauce to squash mixture. Bring to boil. Reduce heat to low and simmer for 10 minutes. Pour into servings bowl. Sprinkle with bacon and cheese.

Note: if the juice is cooked down in this recipe, it is wonderful served on pizza crust and topped with Kraft fat free Mozzarella cheese.

Cranberry Carrots

Servings: 4　　　　**Fat Grams: 0**

6 med. carrots, peeled, sliced crosswise 1/2-inch thick
1/4 c. liquid Butter Buds
1/4 c. jellied cranberry sauce
2 T. brown sugar

Cook carrots until tender. Drain. Coat non-stick skillet with cooking spray. Combine Butter Buds, cranberry sauce, and brown sugar. Stir. Heat on low, stirring until cranberry sauce melts. Add drained carrots. Heat on low until carrots are glazed on all sides.

Easy Sweet Potatoes

Servings: 4   **Fat Grams: 0**

2 (15 oz.) cans sweet potatoes, drained and mashed
2 T. liquid Butter Buds
3/4 c. brown sugar, packed
1/8 tsp. nutmeg
1/8 tsp. cinnamon
8 lg. marshmallows

Coat large non-stick skillet with cooking spray. Combine mashed sweet potatoes, liquid butter buds, brown sugar and nutmeg. Stir well. Pour potato mixture into prepared skillet. Cook over medium heat for 25 minutes. Stir occasionally. The last 5 minutes, push half of the marshmallows into the sweet potatoes. Arrange the others on top. Sprinkle cinnamon on top of the marshmallows. Cover. Reduce heat to low. Cook just until marshmallows melt.

Entrees &
Side Dishes

"You do what you can for as long as you can, and when you finally
can't , you do the next best thing. You back up but you don't give up."

— **Charles "Chuck" Yeager**

Fat Zapping Ideas

• When cooking ground turkey, reduce the fat content even more by draining the meat using a colander. Rinse meat with hot water to remove excess fat. Before returning meat to the skillet be sure to rinse it out as well. Practice this for all your ground meats.

• Pork tenderloin contain the same amount of fat as a whole skinned chicken breast, 4 grams per 4 ounce serving. Slice pork tenderloin to resemble pork ribs. Grill with plenty of barbecue sauce. Enjoy.

• When purchasing beef, keep this in mind. Top round and sirloin cuts generally contain less fat than the other cuts of beef. Remove all visible fat from meat before cooking.

• Divide fat free hot dogs into individual sandwich bags. Freeze in large zip lock freezer safe bag. They are ready to use individually anytime.

• Broth taken from chicken, beef, or pork can be quite tasty used in making gravies or sauces and it can contain little or no fat. Simply place broth in refrigerator; when it cools the fat remains at the top. Remove the fat and use the broth guilt free.

• Guilt Free methods of preparing meats -- poach, bake, steam, microwave, grill, or stir fry.

• Practically all varieties of shellfish are very low in fat. Do not think you have to give up dipping crab or lobster in butter. Liquid Butter Buds and I Can't Believe It's Not Butter spray are the answer. Tartar sauce is a cinch using fat free Miracle Whip salad dressing, white vinegar, and sweet relish.

• Mashed Potatoes, instant or real, taste wonderful whipped using fat free chicken broth or canned evaporated non fat skim milk. Sprinkle on parsley flakes to add eye appeal.

• Thicken soups and sauces with either cornstarch or instant mashed potato flakes; neither contain fat.

Golden Baked Chicken
"Scrumptious"

Servings: 6   **Fat Grams: 3**

6 med. whole chicken breasts, skinned
4 c. crispy rice cereal
   (Place cereal in large ziplock bag and crush with a
   rolling pin.)
2/3 c. liquid Butter Buds
1 tsp. salt, optional
1/2 tsp. pepper

Preheat oven to 350 degrees. Coat shallow baking pan with cooking spray. Place liquid Butter Buds, salt, and pepper into dipping bowl. Dip chicken in butter bud mixture and roll in crumb mixture. Lay chicken in prepared pan. Bake in oven for 1 hour.

Note: Do not cover pan or turn chicken during baking time.

Delectable Crispy Chicken
"Simply Wonderful!"

Servings: 4   **Fat Grams: 4**

4 c. crispy rice cereal
1 c. Kraft fat free Miracle Whip salad dressing
1 envelope Hidden Valley ranch salad dressing mix
1/4 tsp. pepper or to taste
4 chicken breasts, skinned
liquid Butter Buds

Preheat oven to 400 degrees. Coat shallow baking pan with cooking spray. Place cereal in large ziplock plastic bag and crush with rolling pin. Combine salad dressing with dry salad dressing mix. Stir well. Wash and pat dry chicken. Saturate each piece with salad dressing mixture. Place one at a time in bag; shake to coat well. Place each piece (not touching) on a prepared pan. Drizzle each piece lightly with liquid Butter Buds. Bake in preheated oven for 35 to 40 minutes or until chicken is crispy and no longer pink.

Baked Chicken and Mushrooms
(Heavenly!)

Servings: 8   **Fat Grams: 5**

8 whole chicken breasts, skinned
1-1/2 lbs. fresh mushrooms, cut in half or fourths,
    depending on size
1/4 c. liquid Butter Buds
2 (10-3/4 oz.) cans Campbell's Healthy Request cream of
    mushroom soup
salt and pepper to taste, optional

Preheat oven to 350 degrees. Coat baking pan with cooking spray. Spread sliced mushrooms on bottom of pan. Place chicken (meat side up) on top of mushrooms. Pour liquid Butter Buds over chicken. Sprinkle chicken with salt and pepper. Bake uncovered for 30 minutes. Remove from oven. Spread undiluted soup on top of chicken. Bake for 30 minutes or until chicken is no longer pink.

Note: Great served with wild rice and French style green beans.

Pepper-Lime Chicken

Servings: 4   **Fat Grams: 4**

4 whole chicken breasts, boned and skinned, rinse and
    pat dry
1/2 tsp. lime peel, finely shredded
1/3 c. lime juice
2 T. olive oil
1 tsp. crushed dried thyme
1 tsp. cracked black pepper
1/2 tsp. garlic salt

Preheat broiler. Mix together all ingredients except chicken.
Set aside. Place chicken pieces on lightly sprayed broiler
rack. Brush each piece with marinade. Broil for 10 minutes; turn. Repeat process until chicken is fully cooked and
no longer pink. Discard any left over marinade.

Hint: This chicken makes a great sandwich!

Curried Orange Chicken
"Rich taste made simple"

Servings: 6   **Fat Grams: 4**

1 c. orange marmalade
1 T. curry powder
1 tsp. salt, optional
6 chicken breasts, skinned, wash and pat dry

Preheat oven to 350 degrees. Coat a 12 x 9 x 2-inch baking dish with cooking spray. Combine marmalade, curry powder, salt, and one-half cup water. Stir. Place chicken breasts in prepared pan. Pour sauce over chicken. Bake in preheated oven for 45 minutes. Baste several times during baking. If sauce begins to stick during baking period, add one-fourth cup of water.

Cranberry Chicken

Servings: 8   **Fat Grams: 4**

5 lb. chicken breasts, skinned
1 (8 oz.) bottle fat free sweet and spicy French salad
    dressing
1 envelope onion soup mix
1 (16 oz.) can whole cranberry sauce
1 (6 oz.) can mandarin oranges, drained (reserve liquid)

Combine dressing, soup mix, cranberry sauce, and mandarin oranges in crock pot. Place chicken in crock pot. Press chicken down into cranberry mixture. Cover and cook on high for 4 to 5 hours. If needed during cooking period, add mandarin orange liquid.

Barbecue Hawaiian Style Chicken
"Mouth Watering"

Servings: 8   Fat Grams: 4

8 whole chicken breasts, boned and skinned
1/4 c. apricot preserves
1/4 c. fat free Russian salad dressing or fat free Catalina
3 T. honey
2 T. dry onion soup mix

Coat microwave safe baking dish with cooking spray. Cook on high for 15 minutes. Turn dish a half turn every 3 minutes. Preheat broiler. Coat broiler rack with cooking spray. Mix preserves, salad dressing, honey, and soup mix. Stir well. Arrange microwaved chicken on prepared broiler rack. Baste thoroughly. Broil for 3 minutes. Turn over and baste the other side. Broil for 2 to 3 minutes. Repeat process until chicken is no longer pink. Discard any unused marinade.

Note: Recipe is wonderful served on a bed of rice.

Peach Chicken With Rice
"Delightful"

Servings: 6   **Fat Grams: 3.66**

6 chicken breasts, boned, skinned, cut in half
1 (8 oz.) can peach slices (lite syrup),
      drained (reserve liquid)
1 tsp. cornstarch
1/8 tsp. ground ginger
1/4 tsp. salt, optional
1 (8 oz.) can sliced water chestnuts, drained
2 c. hot cooked rice
1 (6 oz.) pkg. frozen snow peas, cooked and drained

Spray a non-stick skillet with cooking spray. Cook chicken until no longer pink. Remove chicken from skillet. Keep warm. Add to reserved liquid if necessary to make one-half cup. Heat liquid in skillet over medium heat. Liquefy cornstarch with water. Add to peach liquid. Stir in ginger and salt. Cook until thick and bubbly. Stir constantly. Turn flame to low. Stir in peaches and water chestnuts. Heat thoroughly. Form a bed of rice on serving platter. Arrange chicken and peas on top of rice. Pour peach sauce over chicken and serve.

Guilt-Free Homemade Chicken and Noodles
"You just won't believe low fat could taste so good."

Servings: 8   Fat Grams: .75

1 whole chicken, cut up leaving skin on
2 c. all-purpose flour
1/2 tsp. salt, optional
1/2 c. egg substitute
1/4 c. skim milk

Place chicken into large pot. Cover chicken with water. Cover and cook chicken until very tender. Remove chicken from broth. Set aside to cool. Remove skin from all white meat. Shred white meat. Refrigerate. Discard the remaining chicken. Pour broth into heat safe bowl. Refrigerate until fat congeals on top. Skim fat. Now all that remains is fat free broth. While broth is chilling, make and dry the noodles. Using a food processor place steel blade in bottom of bowl. Add flour, salt, and egg substitute. Pulse. The consistency should resemble cornmeal. Turn on machine slowly and add skim milk. Continue this process until ball forms. Divide dough in two pieces. Remove from bowl and place on floured surface; cover. Let stand 10 minutes. Roll dough to form two 16 x 12-inch rectangles. Let stand for 20 minutes. Roll up in jelly roll fashion. Slice 1/4-inch wide noodles. Unroll and spread out on clean towels for 2 hours to dry. After 1-1/2 hours, bring fat free broth to a boil. Drop noodles into boiling broth. Stir frequently and cook for 12 minutes or until noodles are tender. Stir in shredded chicken. You may need to thicken broth with cornstarch. Note: Make a runny paste using small amount of water and cornstarch. This will prevent lumps from forming.

Roast Chicken

Servings: 6   **Fat Grams: 3**

6 whole chicken breasts, skinned
6 med. size potatoes, peeled (new if available)
6 lg. carrots, peeled and cut in half
6 small onions, cut in half
2 (14-1/2 oz.) cans fat free chicken broth
pepper to taste
1/4 c. liquid Butter Buds
2 (15 oz.) cans cut green beans

Preheat oven to 350 degrees. Place raised rack in bottom of roaster. Place chicken in middle of roaster. Add vegetables around sides of roaster. Sprinkle all with pepper and drizzle liquid Butter Buds over vegetables. Cover and bake in preheated oven for 2 hours. Save liquid. Thicken with cornstarch and season to taste for a mouthwatering low fat gravy.

Fancy Chicken Casserole

Servings: 4   Fat Grams: 1.67

2 c. Yolk Free dumpling noodles
1 c. boneless chicken breasts, skinned and diced
1/2 c. nonfat sour cream
1 (10-3/4 oz.) can Campbell's Healthy Request
         cream of chicken soup
1/2 tsp. sage
1 tsp. salt, optional
1/2 tsp. pepper
dried parsley flakes

Preheat oven to 350 degrees. Coat baking dish with cooking spray. Cook noodles according to package directions (omitting salt and oil) until almost tender. Combine all ingredients into prepared baking dish. Bake in preheated oven for 30 to 40 minutes or until chicken and noodles are fully cooked. Sprinkle parsley flakes on top.

Chicken Casserole
"Very Good"

Servings: 12   **Fat Grams: 1.5**

6 c. cooked, skinned chicken breasts, diced
2 c. celery, diced
1/2 c. yellow onion, diced
2 (10-3/4 oz.) can Campbell's Healthy Request
    cream of chicken soup
1 tsp. salt, optional
2-1/3 c. Minute Rice
2 T. lemon juice
3 hard boiled eggs (discard yolks, dice whites)
1-1/2 c. Kraft fat free Miracle Whip salad dressing
1 c. Kellogg's Special K cereal

Preheat oven to 375 degrees. Coat a 13 x 9 x 2-inch baking pan with cooking spray. Combine all ingredients into bowl except cereal. Stir. Turn into prepared pan and sprinkle cereal on top. Bake in oven for 45 minutes.

Baked Chicken and Rice
"A Family Favorite"

Servings: 6   **Fat Grams: 3**

6 whole chicken breasts, skinned
1 c. uncooked rice
2 c. skim milk
1 (10-3/4 oz.) can Campbell's Healthy Request
      cream of mushroom soup
1 envelope onion soup mix
paprika

Preheat oven to 350 degrees. Coat a 13 x 9 x 2-inch pan with cooking spray. Combine all ingredients in bowl except chicken. Stir. Pour rice mixture into prepared pan. Place chicken on top. Sprinkle lightly with paprika. cover and bake in preheated oven for 1-1/2 hours. Make sure chicken is no longer pink.

Nutty Broccoli Chicken
"Sooo Good"

Servings: 6   **Fat Grams: 2**

2 c. skinned chicken breasts, cooked and diced
1 (10-3/4 oz.) can Campbell's Healthy Request cream of chicken soup
1/2 soup can of skim milk
2 (10 oz.) pkgs. frozen broccoli, cooked (follow package directions)
1/2 c. Kraft fat free Miracle Whip salad dressing
2 tsp. lemon juice
1/4 c. water chestnuts, drained and slivered

Preheat oven to 350 degrees. Coat baking pan with cooking spray. Layer in prepared pan chicken and broccoli. Combine soup, skim milk, salad dressing, and lemon juice. Whisk. Pour soup mixture over ingredients in pan. Sprinkle water chestnuts on top. Bake uncovered in oven for 30 minutes or until thick and bubbly and chicken is no longer pink.

Rich Turkey 'n Noodle Bake

Servings: 6   Fat Grams: 1.0

3 c. Yolk Free dumpling noodles
1 lb. ground turkey breast
1/2 c. onion, chopped
1/4 c. green bell pepper, chopped
1 (15 oz.) can tomato sauce
1/2 tsp. seasoned salt
1/4 tsp. pepper
2 c. nonfat cream style cottage cheese
1 (3 oz.) pkg. nonfat cream cheese, softened

Preheat oven to 350 degrees. Coat 10 x 6 x 2-inch baking dish with cooking spray. Cook noodles following package directions omitting salt and oil. Drain. Add 1/4 c. water, ground turkey, onion, and bell pepper to non-stick skillet. Cook turkey until fully done and onion is tender. Drain using colander. Rinse with water to remove excess fat. Place meat mixture in bowl. Stir in tomato sauce, seasoned salt, and pepper. Set aside. Blend in separate bowl cottage cheese and cream cheese; beat until fluffy. Add 1 teaspoon of cornstarch to cheese mixture to keep cream cheese from separating. Spoon cooked noodles into prepared baking dish. Spread cheese mixture over noodles. Add meat sauce and spread on top. Bake uncovered for 30 to 40 minutes or until heated thoroughly.

Pigs In A Blanket
"Quick and easy all time favorite"

Servings: 4   **Fat Grams: 1.5**

1 (7.5 oz.) can refrigerator biscuits
    (1.5 fat grams per 2 biscuits)
1 (14 oz.) pkg. Hormel fat free hot-dogs
mustard or honey mustard

Set oven temperature following biscuit directions. Wrap one biscuit around each hot-dog. Leave hot-dogs exposed at each end. Bake. Serve hot. Dip in mustard.

Fantastic Turkey Patties

Servings: 8   **Fat Grams: 1.75**

1 lb. ground turkey breast
1 c. corn flakes, crushed
1 c. tomatoes, crushed
1/4 c. egg substitute
1 sm. onion, minced
1 tsp. salt, optional
1/4 tsp. pepper
8 slices turkey bacon
toothpicks

Mix together ground turkey, corn flakes, tomatoes, egg substitute, salt, pepper. Shape into one-inch thick patties. Wrap slice of bacon around each patty; fasten with toothpick. Place patties on broiler rack about 3 inches from heat. Broil for 10 minutes. Turn and broil until other side is brown.

Tortilla and Green Chile Casserole
"A favorite in our house!"

Servings: 6   Fat Grams: 5

2 lb. ground turkey breast
1/2 c. onion, chopped
1 (15 oz.) can tomato sauce
1 envelope of taco seasoning
1-1/2 T. chili powder (if you like it hot)
1 (8 oz.) can green chilies (less according to taste)
salt to taste, optional
1/4 c. black olives, sliced
1 c. salsa, chunky style
12 corn tortillas
2 (10-3/4 oz.) cans Campbell's Healthy Request cream of
   mushroom soup
1 soup can of skim milk
2 c. Kraft fat free shredded cheddar cheese

Preheat oven to 350 degrees. Coat a 12 x 7 1/2 x 2-inch baking pan with cooking spray. Crumble and cook turkey and onion in 1/4 c. water. Drain using a colander. Rinse with water to remove excess fat. Rinse skillet and dry. Place in skillet turkey mixture, tomato sauce, taco seasoning, chili powder, green chilies, and black olives. Heat until thick and bubbly. Whisk together in bowl the soup and skim milk. Pour salsa into bottom of prepared pan. Spread out 6 tortillas over salsa. Spoon one-half of meat mixture and one-half cheese over tortillas. Repeat layers except for salsa. Pour soup mixture over top. Sprinkle remaining cheese on top. Bake in oven for 30 to 35 minutes. Serve with salsa and nonfat sour cream.

Chicken Pan Enchilada
"You won't have to beg 'em to eat this one!"

Servings: 5   Fat Grams: 6.8

4 chicken breasts, skinned, boned, pounded flat,
    cut into strips
1 envelope taco seasoning
1/2 c. water
1/2 c. chunky picante sauce or chunky salsa
10 corn tortillas (1 fat gram each)
2 (10 -3/4 oz.) cans Campbell's Healthy Request
    cream of mushroom soup
1 (8 oz.) pkg. Kraft fat free shredded Cheddar cheese
2 T. chopped green chilies, optional
nonfat sour cream
salsa

Using large non-stick skillet brown chicken in butter flavor cooking spray until no longer pink. Preheat oven to 350 degrees. Coat a 12 x 9-inch baking pan with butter flavor cooking spray. Stir in skillet taco seasoning and water. Simmer for 4 minutes. Spread picante sauce evenly in bottom of prepared pan. Add equal amounts of chicken to tortillas. Roll and place seam side down on bottom of pan. Pour remaining taco seasoning sauce over filled tortillas. Spread mushroom soup evenly over top. Sprinkle cheese on top, then green chilies if desired. cover tightly with foil. Bake in preheated oven for 20 minutes. Uncover and bake for 10 to 12 minutes longer. Make sure cheese does not burn. Serve with nonfat sour cream and salsa.

Tex-Mex Chicken and Rice
"Very Eye-Appealing!"

Servings: 6   **Fat Grams: 4.66**

6 whole chicken breasts, boned, skinned, halved
1 T. olive oil
1 onion, chopped
1 sm. green bell pepper, chopped
1 clove garlic, minced
1 (14-1/2 oz.) can Del Monte Mexican Recipe
    stewed tomatoes
1 (14-1/2 oz.) can chicken broth
1-3/4 c. quick cooking rice
few drops hot sauce, optional
1/2 c. Kraft fat free shredded cheddar cheese
2 T. black olives, chopped
nonfat sour cream/salsa

Preheat oven to 350 degrees. Coat a 2-quart casserole with cooking spray. Using a non-stick skillet brown chicken in oil for 2 minutes on each side. Remove browned chicken and set aside. Combine in same skillet onion, pepper, and garlic. You may need to add a small amount of water for sautéing. Cook but do not brown. Stir into onion mixture tomatoes, broth, uncooked rice, and hot sauce. Cover and bring mixture to boil. Pour rice mixture into prepared casserole. Arrange browned chicken on top. Bake in preheated oven for 30 to 35 minutes or until rice is fully cooked. Garnish with cheese, olives, and nonfat sour cream.

Tex-Mex Meat Loaf

Servings: 4   **Fat Grams: 1.5**

1 lb. ground turkey breast
1 c. frozen corn, thawed
1/3 c. lowest fat bread crumbs
1 small onion, chopped
3/4 c. mild salsa
1/4 tsp. garlic powder
1/4 c. egg substitute
1 tsp. chili powder
1 tsp. salt, optional
1/4 tsp. pepper
1/4 c. mild salsa (reserve)
1 tsp. black olives, chopped (reserve)

Preheat oven to 350 degrees. Coat loaf pan with cooking spray. Mix with hands all ingredients except salsa and black olives. Bake in preheated oven for 35 minutes. Pour reserved salsa on top and bake the last 10 minutes. Remove from oven and sprinkle olives on top.

Spicy Tex-Mex Topper
for Tostadas, Pizza, Pita Sandwich, Rice, etc.

Servings: 8   **Fat Grams: 0.5**

1 lb. ground turkey breast
1 envelope taco seasoning
1 (14.5 oz.) can diced tomatoes and green chilies
    with onions
1 (15 oz.) can dark kidney beans, drained and rinsed
1/2 of 4 oz. can diced greens chilies (more if desired)
1 (11 oz.) can shoepeg corn

Brown ground turkey in large non-stick skillet. Drain using a colander. Rinse meat with water. Rinse skillet with water. Return turkey to skillet. Combine taco seasoning with 1/2 cup water. Simmer over medium heat for 3 minutes. Stir in tomatoes, beans, green chilies, and corn. Continue to simmer for 20 minutes. Choose your method of serving this topping. Don't forget to include Kraft fat free shredded cheddar cheese, nonfat sour cream, and salsa. Enjoy!

Easy Chicken Fajitas
"We love them!"

Servings: 6   **Fat Grams: 2.4**

3 whole chicken breasts, boned and skinned,
      cut into thin strips
1/2 c. water
1 envelope taco seasoning
1 lg. green bell pepper, halved, seeded,
      and cut into thin strips
1 med. onion, halved, cut into thin strips
12 (6-inch) fat free flour tortillas
1 c. Kraft fat free shredded Cheddar cheese
nonfat sour cream

Place chicken strips, water, and taco seasoning into small bowl. Set aside. Sauté peppers and onions in non-stick skillet using cooking spray. You may need to add a small amount of water to skillet. Sauté, leaving peppers and onions a little crunchy. Set aside. Using same skillet add chicken mixture marinade included. Cook until chicken is no longer pink and liquid is almost gone. Place tortillas in microwave safe covered dish. Microwave on high for 30 seconds. Keep the lid on tortillas during serving time. Combine on half the tortillas the chicken, onions, peppers, cheese, and sour cream. Fold in half. It's messy, but it's worth it!

Fajitas On-A-Stick

Servings: 4   **Fat Grams: 4.25**

3 chicken breasts, skinned, boned, cut into
      medium strips
8 (9-in.) bamboo skewers
8 (6-in.) fat free flour tortillas
1/3 c. fat free Italian dressing
3 T. fresh lime juice
2 med. green or red bell peppers, seeded,
      and cut lengthwise into quarters
1 med. onion cut into 1-in. square wedges
salsa

Soak skewers in water for at lest 10 minutes. Alternate pieces of chicken with peppers and onions on skewers. Marinate loaded skewers in dressing and lime juice mixture for 30 minutes. (Marinated chicken needs to be kept in refrigerator.) Wrap tortillas in foil. Place skewers over hot coals for 8 to 10 minutes or until chicken is no longer pink. Turn to ensure even cooking. Set wrapped tortillas on one side of grill for 5 minutes or until heated. Wrap tortillas around skewers. Hold tightly and pull out skewer. Top with salsa and enjoy.

Chicko Taco
"Super"

Servings: 6   **Fat Grams: 4.4**

3 whole chicken breasts, boned, skinned,
    and cut into thin strips
1/2 c. water
1 envelope taco seasoning
12 taco shells (Taco Bell = 2 fat grams per 2 shells)
1 (15 oz.) can fat free refried beans
1 c. Kraft fat free shredded Cheddar cheese
1/2 head lettuce, shredded
1 lg. tomato, diced
nonfat sour cream
salsa

Add chicken, water, and taco seasoning to non-stick skillet. Cook until chicken is no longer pink and liquid is almost gone. Place shells in microwave safe covered dish. Microwave on high for 30 to 45 seconds. Keep lid on during serving. Spread 1 tablespoon of refried beans on inside half of shell. Add 3 strips of chicken, Cheddar cheese, lettuce, and tomato. Top off with salsa and a dollop of nonfat sour cream. Enjoy with no guilt.

Taco Turkey Burgers
"Quick and Tasty"

Servings: 8   **Fat Grams: 1.5**

1 lb. ground turkey breast
1 (16 oz.) can chopped tomatoes
1 tsp. chili powder
1 tsp. Worcestershire sauce (reduced sodium)
3/4 tsp. garlic salt, optional
1/2 tsp. sugar
1/4 tsp. dry mustard
2 c. shredded lettuce
1 c. Kraft fat free shredded Cheddar cheese
1 pkg. of 8 hamburger buns
salsa

Brown ground turkey with a small amount of water. Drain using a colander. Rinse with water to remove excess fat. Rinse skillet with water and dry. Return turkey to skillet. Add all ingredients except lettuce and cheese. Bring to bubbly stage. Reduce heat. Simmer uncovered until thick and bubbly. Heat buns in microwave 30 seconds. Place meat mixture on bottom bun, followed by lettuce, cheese and top bun. Serve with salsa if desired.

Mexican Stuffed Peppers

Servings: 6   **Fat Grams: Less than 1**

6 med. green bell peppers, tops cut off and seeded
1 lb. ground turkey breast
1 lg. yellow onion, chopped
1-1/3 c. fresh tomato, peeled and chopped
1 c. elbow macaroni, cooked and drained
1 tsp. salt, optional
1 tsp. chili powder
1 (8 oz.) can tomato sauce

Preheat oven to 375 degrees. Coat shallow 2-quart casserole with cooking spray. Place peppers in boiling water for 5 minutes. Drain and set aside. Combine in bowl the rest of ingredients except tomato sauce. Mix well. Fill peppers with turkey mixture. Place filled peppers in prepared casserole. Pour tomato sauce on top and around sides of peppers. Bake for 45 to 50 minutes.

Spicy Meal-In-One Potatoes

Servings: 4   **Fat Grams: 1**

1 lb. ground turkey breast
2 lg. baking potatoes
1/2 c. onion, chopped
1 (12 oz.) jar chunky picante sauce or salsa
1/2 tsp. salt, optional
2 slices fat free cheese, cut diagonally into quarters
1 green onion, sliced

Scrub potatoes and remove any imperfections. Using fork prick several holes in potatoes. Cook in microwave on high for 8 to 10 minutes. Rotate potatoes one-fourth turn after 4 minutes. Let stand. Combine ground turkey and onion in non-stick skillet. Cook until turkey is fully done. You may need to use cooking spray or small amount of water (1/4 cup) to cook turkey. Drain in colander and rinse with water to remove excess fat. Rinse skillet with water and dry with paper towels. Return meat mixture to skillet and add picante sauce. Stir and heat thoroughly. Cut potatoes lengthwise in half. Fluff inside using a fork. Sprinkle each half with salt, if desired. Spoon equal amounts of turkey mixture over each potato. Top each with equal amounts of cheese. Place in microwave for a few seconds to melt cheese. Garnish with green onion slices. Serve stuffed potatoes with a tossed green salad and fat free dressing. Offer toasted French bread lightly sprayed with I Can't Believe It's Not Butter Spray. Enjoy!

Chicken Tortilla Pizzas
"Quick-Fun-Delicious"

Yield: 4 pizzas

Fat Grams: 4.81 with low fat cheese; 2.31 with fat free cheese

4 (6-inch) corn tortillas
1 (16 oz.) can fat free refried beans
1 c. skinned, cooked, chicken breast strips, fried in butter spray
1/4 c. sliced green onions, tips included
2 T. sliced ripe olives
2 T. sliced pimiento
4 oz. or 1/2 c. low fat shredded Monterey Jack cheese or fat free shredded Cheddar cheese
Guilt Free Guacamole (See Appetizer Section)
nonfat sour cream
picante sauce or salsa

Preheat oven to 400 degrees. Arrange tortillas on ungreased cookie sheet. Lightly spray tortillas with butter flavor cooking spray. Bake tortillas for 5 minutes or just until crisp but not brown. Place equal amounts of refried beans, chicken strips, onions, olives, pimiento, and cheese on tortillas. (End with cheese on top.) Bake for 10 minutes or just until cheese melts. Garnish with fat free guacamole, sour cream, or picante sauce.

Mama's Lasagna

Servings: 8   **Fat Grams: 1**

1 lb. ground turkey breast
3/4 T. onion, chopped
1 (16 oz.) can tomatoes
2 (6 oz.) cans tomato paste
2 c. water
1 T. parsley, ground
2 tsp. salt, optional
1 tsp. sugar
1 tsp. garlic powder
1/2 tsp. pepper
1/2 tsp. oregano
1 (16 oz.) pkg. lasagna noodles, cooked and drained
(omit oil and salt in cooking noodles)
1 (16 oz.) carton nonfat Ricotta cheese
1 (16 oz.) pkg. Kraft fat free shredded Mozzarella cheese
Kraft fat free grated Parmesan cheese topping

Brown turkey and onion in a non-stick skillet sprayed with butter flavor cooking spray. Drain using colander. Rinse with water to remove any excess fat. Rinse skillet with water and dry. Return meat mixture to skillet. Add to mixture in skillet tomatoes, tomato paste, water, parsley, salt, sugar, garlic powder, pepper, and oregano. Simmer over low heat for 45 minutes. Preheat oven to 350 degrees. Coat a 13 x 9 x 2-inch baking pan with cooking spray. Layer in prepared baking pan noodles, sauce, Ricotta cheese, and Mozzarella cheese. Repeat layers ending with Mozzarella cheese on top. Bake in oven for 30 to 45 minutes. Serve with grated Parmesan cheese topping.

Same Skillet Lasagna
"Very appetizing and quick!"

Servings: 4   **Fat Grams: 3.25**

6 lasagna noodles, broken
1 c. nonfat cream style cottage cheese
4 oz. nonfat cream cheese
      (with 1 tsp. cornstarch stirred into the cheese)
1/2 c. Kraft fat free Mozzarella cheese
1/4 c. Kraft nonfat grated Parmesan Cheese
1/2 tsp. Italian seasoning
3/4 lb. ground turkey breast
1 clove garlic, minced
1 (15-1/2 oz.) can spaghetti sauce
      (Hunts has .5 fat grams per serving)
1/2 c. Kraft fat free Mozzarella cheese
2 T. Kraft nonfat grated Parmesan Cheese topping

Cook broken lasagna noodles for 12 minutes in boiling water; omit salt and oil. Drain. Combine cottage cheese, cream cheese, Mozzarella cheese, Parmesan cheese, and Italian seasoning. Stir well. Set aside. In dutch oven cook turkey and garlic in 1/4 cup water. Drain. Return to dutch oven. Stir spaghetti sauce and cooked noodles into turkey mixture. Add cottage cheese mixture to top of mixture in dutch oven. Next sprinkle Mozzarella and then Parmesan cheese topping. Cover and reduce heat to low. Cook until heated thoroughly.

Spaghetti Pizza Bake

Servings: 8   **Fat Grams: 2**

1 (16 oz.) pkg. spaghetti, broken into 3-inch pieces
    (cook without salt and oil, drain, and cool)
1/2 c. egg substitute, lightly beaten
3/4 c. skim milk
4 c. Kraft fat free shredded Mozzarella cheese, divided
1/2 tsp. salt, optional
4 c. zero fat spaghetti sauce
1-1/2 tsp. oregano
1 (3-1/2 oz.) pkg. reduced fat Hormel turkey
    pepperoni slices

Preheat oven to 350 degrees. Coat a 15 x 10-inch jelly roll pan with cooking spray. Combine egg substitute, milk, one cup of the Mozzarella cheese, and salt in large bowl. Toss in spaghetti. Stir well making sure noodles are evenly coated with cheese mixture. Pour spaghetti mixture into prepared pan. Top with spaghetti sauce, spreading evenly. Sprinkle oregano and remaining Mozzarella cheese over sauce. Arrange pepperoni slices on top. Bake for 30 to 45 minutes. Let stand for 5 minutes before serving.

Spaghetti In A Pan

Servings: 6   **Fat Grams: 2.17**

2 lbs. ground turkey breast
6 green onions, chopped
1 (10-3/4 oz.) can tomato soup
1 (15 oz.) can tomato sauce
4 oz. Kraft fat free shredded Cheddar cheese
3/4 lb. Healthy Choice process cheese, cubed
1 (12 oz.) pkg. spaghetti
      (cooked without salt and oil, drained)
1 (10-3/4 oz.) can Campbell's Healthy Request
      cream of mushroom soup

Preheat oven to 450 degrees. Coat a 13 x 9 x 2-inch pan with cooking spray. Cook turkey and onions in 1/4 cup of water. Drain using colander. Rinse with water to remove excess fat. Rinse skillet with water and dry. Return turkey mixture to skillet. Stir in tomato soup, tomato sauce, and both cheeses. Continue to stir until both cheeses have melted. Stir in cooked spaghetti. Pour spaghetti mixture into prepared pan. Spread soup over top. Bake for 45 minutes. Let stand 5 minutes before serving.

Chicken-Filled Shells

Servings: 8   **Fat Grams: 2.75**

2 c. chicken breasts, skinned, cooked, and diced
1 c. frozen peas, cooked, and drained
1/2 c. Kraft fat free Miracle Whip salad dressing
1/3 c. onion, finely chopped
salt (optional) and pepper to taste
1 (12 oz.) pkg. jumbo shell macaroni, cooked, drained
1/2 c. water
1 (10-3/4 oz.) can Campbell's Healthy Request
     cream of mushroom soup

Preheat oven to 325 degrees. Coat baking dish with cooking spray. Combine in bowl cooked chicken, peas, salad dressing, onion, salt, and pepper. Stir well. Fill chicken mixture to top of shells. Arrange shells in prepared baking dish. Mix water and soup together. Pour soup mixture over shells. Cover tightly with foil. Bake in preheated oven for 30 minutes.

Cheese Manicotti
"Quick and easy—don't tell your secret!"

Servings: 4   **Fat Grams: 2.5**

8 manicotti shells (lowest in fat)
1/2 c. nonfat small curd cottage cheese
1/4 c. Kraft fat free grated Parmesan cheese topping
1/4 c. egg substitute
1/2 c. fresh parsley, chopped fine
black pepper to taste
1 (26-1/2 oz.) can Hunt's Spaghetti Sauce
          with Mushrooms

Preheat oven to 350 degrees. Coat baking dish with cooking spray. Cook manicotti shells for 8 minutes in boiling water without oil or salt. Drain and cool to the touch. Combine cottage cheese, Parmesan cheese, egg substitute, parsley, and pepper. Stir well. Stuff each shell with cheese mixture. Place lengthwise in prepared baking dish. Pour spaghetti sauce over top. Cover with foil and bake in oven for 15 minutes. Remove cover and bake 15 more minutes. Serve with salad and lowest fat garlic bread.

Garlic Butter 'n Fettuccine

Servings: 4   **Fat Grams: 1.5 without pine nuts**
5.25 with pine nuts

1 (8 oz.) pkg. fettuccine, cooked and drained
(without salt or oil)
1/4 c. liquid Butter Buds
1 T. pine nuts
2 cloves garlic, crushed
pinch of Italian herb seasoning
1/4 c. Kraft fat free grated Parmesan cheese topping

Brown pine nuts in non-stick skilled using butter flavor cooking spray. Remove from skillet and set aside. Combine garlic, liquid Butter Buds, and herb seasoning in microwave safe bowl. Add cooked pasta to butter mixture. Toss well to coat. Heat in microwave until thoroughly heated. Top with pine nuts and sprinkle each serving with grated Parmesan cheese topping.

Mushroom Fettuccine

Servings: 4   **Fat Grams: 4.75**

1 (10-1/2 oz.) can Campbell's Healthy Request
cream of mushroom soup
3/4 c. skim milk
1/4 c. grated Parmesan cheese (1 fat gram per tablespoon)
3 c. cooked fettuccine (omit oil and salt when cooking)
1/4 c. liquid Butter Buds
Kraft fat free grated Parmesan cheese topping

Heat soup and milk in large non-stick skillet. Blend in Parmesan cheese. Stir to melt cheese. Add liquid Butter Buds; stir to blend. Add cooked fettuccine. Toss well to coat. Serve with Parmesan cheese.

Fettuccine with Mushroom and Asparagus Sauce

Servings: 4   Fat Grams: 3.25

12 oz. fettuccine
1 lb. asparagus, trimmed and cut into 1-inch diagonals
4 T. liquid Butter Buds
2 c. fresh mushrooms, chopped
1/4 c. onion chopped
1 clove garlic, crushed
3/4 c. Land O' Lakes fat free half-and-half
2 tsp. pine nuts (toasted in hot non-stick skillet and
          cooked about 1 minute)
2 T. Kraft fat free grated Parmesan cheese topping

Cook pasta following package directions, omitting salt and oil. Steam asparagus until crisp, but tender. Sauté mushrooms and onions in large non-stick skillet with liquid Butter Buds and 1/4 cup of water until crisp tender. Drain most of liquid. Add garlic and sauté for 1 more minute. Drain. Stir half and half into skillet and heat until boiling. Turn off heat. Stir in asparagus. Toss in hot pasta, pine nuts, and cheese.

Fettuccine with Primavera Sauce
"Quick and hearty dish."

Servings: 4   Fat Grams: 1

12 oz. traditional fettuccine
2 T. liquid Butter Buds
3 T. water
1 (16 oz.) pkg. frozen Italian-style vegetables
1/3 c. Land O' Lakes fat free half-and-half
1/2 c. Kraft fat free grated Parmesan cheese topping
1/2 sm. pkg. cherry tomatoes, rinsed
1 T. flat leaf parsley, chopped

Cook pasta following package directions, omitting salt and oil. Combine in non-stick skillet Butter Buds and water. Stir in frozen vegetables. Cook over low heat for 5 minutes or until vegetables are tender. Beat half and half and Parmesan cheese in serving bowl. Drain pasta well. Place hot pasta in serving bowl with cheese mixture. Toss pasta to coat. Add cooked vegetables, cherry tomatoes, and parsley. Toss well. Serve immediately.

Quick Noodle Dinner

Servings: 4   Fat Grams: 3

1 lb. ground turkey breast
1 T. dried onion flakes
1 (10-3/4 oz.) can Campbell's Healthy Request
    cream of chicken soup
1/2 c. skim milk
1/2 tsp. sage
2 c. Yolk Free egg noodles, uncooked

Brown turkey in large non-stick skillet. Drain using a colander. Rinse with water to remove excess fat. Rinse skillet with water and dry. Return meat to skillet. Add dried onion, soup, milk, sage, and uncooked noodles. Stir and cover. Cook over low heat for 30 minutes. Stir occasionally.

Stroganoff

Servings: 6   Fat Grams: 2.75

1/2 lb. ground turkey breast
1 (14.5 oz.) can beef broth, low sodium
1 tsp. minced onion
1 (8 oz.) pkg. small egg noodles (lowest in fat)
1 (10-3/4 oz.) can Campbell's Healthy Request
    cream of mushroom with cracked pepper
    and herb soup
2 soup cans water

Brown ground turkey in large non-stick skillet. Drain using a colander. Rinse meat with water. Rinse skillet with water to remove excess fat. Return skillet to flame. Add beef broth and onion. Stir in noodles. Cook until noodles are almost tender. Stir in soup, water and meat. Simmer until noodles are fully cooked.

Cheese Frankfurter Casserole
Very Low Fat

Servings: 6   Fat Grams: 2 in entire recipe

3/4 c. elbow macaroni
   (omit oil and salt when cooking)
6 Hormel fat free hot-dogs
1/3 c. onion, chopped
1/3 c. green bell pepper, chopped
2 T. liquid Butter Buds
3 T. all-purpose flour
1 tsp. Worcestershire sauce
1/2 tsp. prepared mustard
1 c. skim milk
1-1/2 c. nonfat cream style cottage cheese

Preheat oven to 350 degrees. Coat 1-1/2 quart casserole with cooking spray. Cook macaroni following package directions. Drain. Slice hot-dogs very thin. Set aside. Sauté onion and bell pepper in liquid butter buds and 1/4 cup water until onions become tender. Drain. Add flour to 2 tablespoons water to form a smooth paste. Stir into onion mixture the flour paste, Worcestershire sauce, mustard, salt, and pepper. Mix well. Whisk in skim milk all at one time. Cook over medium heat stirring constantly until thick and bubbly. Blend in hot-dogs, macaroni, and nonfat cottage cheese. Pour into prepared baking dish. Bake uncovered for 20 minutes. Stir mixture once. Cut the two remaining hot-dogs into thirds diagonally. Place on top of casserole. Bake until thoroughly heated.

Goulash

Servings: 4   **Fat Grams: 2**

1 lb. ground turkey breast
1 c. yellow onion, chopped
1 clove garlic, crushed
3 c. Yolk Free egg noodles or elbow macaroni, uncooked
1 (20 oz.) can tomato juice
1-1/2 tsp. reduced sodium Worcestershire sauce
1-1/2 tsp. celery salt
1/8 tsp. black pepper
1 tsp. salt, optional
1 (10-3/4 oz.) can fat free beef broth, low sodium
1/2 c. water
1/3 c. green bell pepper, seeded and chopped
1 c. nonfat sour cream
1 (4 oz.) can sliced mushrooms, drained

In large non-stick skillet brown turkey, onion, and garlic over medium heat. Drain using a colander. Rinse meat mixture with water to remove excess fat. Rinse out skillet with water and dry. Place turkey mixture back into non-stick skillet. Stir in dry noodles, tomato juice, Worcestershire sauce, celery salt, black pepper, salt, beef broth, and water. Cover and simmer over low heat for 20 minutes. Stir occasionally. Add bell peppers. Simmer until noodles become tender, approximately 10 minutes. Cook for 4 more minutes. Add sour cream and mushrooms. Reheat for 5 minutes, stirring frequently.

This recipe is dedicated to my brother Donald Gene who loves goulash as much today as he did when he was a kid. Just don't tell him that when he eats at Sissy's house, it's low fat.

Poppy Seed Noodles

Servings: 4   **Fat Grams: 1**

1 (8 oz.) pkg. Yolk Free egg noodles, cooked and drained
   (omit salt and oil when cooking noodles)
1 to 2 T. liquid Butter Buds
2 tsp. poppy seeds

Combine cooked, drained noodles in serving dish. Toss with liquid Butter Buds and poppy seeds. Serve immediately.

Cheese 'n Tuna Casserole
"Guilt Free"

Servings: 4   **Fat Grams: Less than 1**

1 (6 oz.) can water packed tuna
1 (10-3/4 oz.) can of Campbell's Healthy Request
   cream of mushroom soup
3 c. crispy rice cereal
1 c. Kraft fat free shredded Cheddar cheese OR
   fat free Best Choice shredded Cheddar cheese

Preheat oven to 350 degrees. Coat a 1-1/2 -quart casserole dish with cooking spray. Combine tuna and soup. Mix well. Fold in rice cereal, one cup at a time. Place in prepared casserole. Bake in preheated oven for 45 minutes. Sprinkle cheese on top and place back in oven just until cheese melts.

Note: Serve with salad and croissant for an extra special low fat meal.

119

Pizza Crust
"Kids can help!"

Makes: 2 crusts

Fat Grams: Less than 1 per crust

1 pkg. active dry yeast
4 c. all-purpose flour
1/2 tsp. salt, optional
1-1/4 c. warm water (115 degrees)
cornmeal

Combine water and yeast in large bowl. Stir to dissolve. Add two cups of flour and salt. Blend flour mixture thoroughly. Add rest of flour and stir in well. Turn onto lightly floured surface. (Important: Knead until smooth. Process will take about 10 minutes. When finished, dough should be smooth and elastic.) Coat bowl with cooking spray. Place dough in bowl, cover, and place in warm area to let rise until doubled in size. Turn onto floured board and knead to force out air bubbles. Divide dough in half. Each pizza half will make an 11-inch pizza. Roll out dough on very lightly floured surface. Coat pizza pans with cooking spray and sprinkle lightly with cornmeal. Place dough on pans. Form crust with fingers or roll out with rolling pin. Sprinkle edges with cornmeal and lightly press into crust. Add nonfat or low fat sauce and toppings. Bake in oven at 450 degrees for 20 to 25 minutes.

Note: Hormel has great low fat pepperoni or use cooked ground turkey breast, canadian bacon, or very low fat ham slices. Use the lowest fat spaghetti sauce you can find. Use vegetables of all types and Kraft fat free grated Parmesan cheese topping and Kraft fat free shredded Mozzarella cheese. (Broil your vegetables first for a richer looking pizza.) Be creative and enjoy!

Easy Wild Rice

Servings: 4   **Fat Grams: 0**

1 c. wild rice
pinch of thyme
salt, optional
1-3/4 c. fat free chicken broth
1/2 bay leaf
freshly ground pepper to taste

In saucepan combine rice, broth, and seasonings. Bring to a full boil. Remove bay leaf. Pour into lightly coated casserole with butter flavor cooking spray. Cover tightly with foil and bake at 375 degrees for 30 minutes or until rice is tender. Drain liquid if there is any left after baking. Toss with fork and serve.

Mushroom Rice Pilaf

Servings: 4   **Fat Grams: 0**

1/2 c. sliced onion
1-1/2 T. parsley, chopped
1/8 tsp. sweet basil
1 (4 oz.) can sliced mushrooms, drained
1-1/2 c. rice (cooked in fat free beef broth)
2 T. liquid Butter Buds

Sauté onions in butter flavor spray in non-stick skillet until onions become transparent and tender. Stir in remaining ingredients. Heat rice mixture thoroughly, stir continuously.

Red Beans and Rice
"Great side dish for any Tex-Mex style meal."

Servings: 4   **Fat Grams: 1.7**

1 c. extra lean 96% fat free fully cooked ham, cubed
1 c. onion, diced
1 c. green bell pepper, diced
1/2 c. celery, diced
2 tsp. garlic, minced
1 to 3 tsp. jalapeño pepper, minced and drained
1 (8 oz.) can red kidney beans, rinsed and drained
1/2 c. tomato or V-8 juice
1/2 tsp. dried oregano
2 c. cooked white rice, hot
2 T. scallions, chopped
2 T. parsley, minced

Coat a non-stick skillet with butter flavor cooking spray. Over medium heat brown ham, onion, bell pepper, celery, garlic, and jalapeño pepper. Cook for 5 minutes until vegetables are crisp tender. Stir in beans, tomato juice, oregano, and 1/4 cup of water. Bring bean mixture to a boil. Simmer over low heat uncovered for 10 minutes. Place rice in serving platter. Spoon bean mixture over hot rice. Sprinkle scallions and parsley over top to garnish. This dish goes well with the Pepper Lime Chicken found in the Entree and Side Dish section of this book.

Shrimp and Rice
"Very Filling"

Servings: 4   Fat Grams: Less than 1

2 T. onion, chopped
1 c. or 4.5 oz. can shrimp
1-1/3 c. Minute Rice
1/2 c. egg substitute, scrambled into small pieces
1 c. Healthy Request chicken broth or fat free
    chicken broth
1 (3 oz.) can mushrooms, undrained
1 c. frozen peas, cooked
1 tsp. soy sauce, reduced sodium

Sauté onion, shrimp, and rice in small amount of chicken broth just until shrimp turns pink. Remove skillet from heat and stir in scrambled eggs. Combine in saucepan remaining chicken broth, mushrooms with liquid, peas, and soy sauce. Bring to boil. Turn off heat. Stir in rice mixture and cover. Let stand for 5 minutes. Toss lightly with fork before serving.

Broiled Salmon
"Beautiful"

Servings: 4   **Fat Grams: 4**

4 (4 oz.) salmon steaks
1/4 c. lemon juice
1 tsp. lemon peel, grated
1 clove garlic, crushed
2 tsp. chopped chives, dried or fresh
1/2 tsp. paprika

Place in a jar with lid the lemon juice, lemon peel, crushed garlic, chives, and paprika; shake. Place salmon steaks in bottom of long shallow dish. Pour marinade over steaks. Cover and refrigerate for 1 hour. Turn steaks over once. Lightly coat broiler racks with cooking spray. Turn on broiler. Remove steaks from marinade. Place on racks 6 inches from flame. Brush steaks with marinade. Cook for 5 minutes. Turn and brush with marinade. Broil for 5 to 8 minutes longer. When done steaks should flake easily with tines of fork.

Jake's Catch-of-the-Day Oven Fried Fish
Recipe for catfish, bass, or perch
(My son Jake, age 11, hopes you enjoy this as much as he does!)

Servings: 6   Fat Grams: trace

Catch of the day (about 2 lbs. of fish)
1 c. skim milk
salt and pepper to taste, optional
4 c. crispy rice cereal, crushed to medium size crumbs
1/2 c. liquid Butter Buds

Preheat oven to 500 degrees. Coat jelly roll pan with butter flavor cooking spray. Dip fillets into salt and pepper seasoned milk. Roll in crushed rice cereal. Coat fish well with crumb mixture. Place on prepared pan. Lightly drizzle liquid Butter Buds over fish. Bake in preheated oven for 15 minutes or until fish flakes easily with tines of fork.

Sweet-Sour Kraut 'n Chops

Servings: 6   **Fat Grams: 7.5**

4 med. baking potatoes, peeled and thinly sliced (4 c.)
1/2 c. onion, chopped
6 lean cut pork chops, all visible fat trimmed
1 (27 oz.) can sauerkraut, drained and rinsed
1 (20 oz.) can crushed pineapple, undrained
2 T. brown sugar
1/2 tsp. salt, optional
dash of pepper

Preheat oven to 350 degrees. Coat a 12 x 7 x 2-inch baking dish with cooking spray. Combine potato slices and onion with 1/4 cup of water in prepared baking dish. Bake covered until nearly tender, about 45 minutes. Meanwhile, using a non-stick skillet and cooking spray brown the chops on both sides. Combine sauerkraut, undrained pineapple, and brown sugar. Spoon over potato mixture. Arrange chops on top. Season with salt and pepper. Cover and bake for 45 minutes.

Sensational Pork 'n Apples with Stuffing

Servings: 8   Fat Grams: 6.33

3 lb. pork tenderloin (cut into 12 slices and flattened)
2 (20 oz.) cans pie-sliced apples, drained
1/2 c. packed brown sugar
6 c. fat free herb-seasoned stuffing mix or 1 fat gram per serving stuffing mix
1/2 c. chopped celery
1/4 c. liquid Butter Buds
3 T. instant minced onion
1 tsp. salt, optional
1/2 tsp. ground sage
2 c. fat free beef broth, low sodium

Preheat oven to 375 degrees. Coat two 12 x 7 x 2-inch baking dishes with cooking spray. In non-stick skillet coated with cooking spray brown meat on both sides well. Place equal amounts of tenderloin into each prepared dish. Stir together apples and brown sugar. Spoon apple mixture over meat. Combine stuffing, celery, liquid butter buds, onion, salt, and sage. Toss with beef broth. Moisten thoroughly. Using measuring cup, press stuffing into 1/2 cup size mounds on each tenderloin. Bake uncovered in oven for 1 hour or until pork is done and tender.

This meal is great if you want to show off just a little.

Scalloped Potatoes and Ham
"Delicious and Filling!"

Servings: 6   Fat Grams: 2.27

2 c. fully cooked 98% fat free ham, cubed
6 c. potatoes, peeled and thinly sliced
1/4 c. onion, finely chopped
1/3 c. all-purpose flour
2 c. skim milk
3 T. fine dry bread crumbs
      (1 fat gram or less per serving)
1 T. liquid Butter Buds
2 T. fresh parsley, snipped or 2 tsp. parsley flakes

Preheat oven to 350 degrees. Coat a 2-quart casserole with cooking spray. Place 1 cup of ham in bottom of casserole. Next layer with half potatoes and half the onions. Repeat layers with remaining ham, flour, potatoes, and onions—ending with flour on top. Pour milk over all. Cover and bake in preheated oven for 1 to 1-1/4 hours or until potatoes are tender. Mix together bread crumbs and liquid butter buds. Sprinkle crumbs on top of casserole. Bake for another 15 minutes.

Breads & Muffins

"You may have to fight a battle more than once to win it."
— **Margaret Thatcher**

More Fat Zapping Ideas

• Always compare labels. Items of the same nature can contain varying degrees of fat. Example: Coffee Creamer. Some brands contain zero fat while others will have as much as 2 fat grams per serving.

• Beware of products that read "lite" or "reduced". Read those labels carefully. It is best to choose low fat or zero fat whenever you can.

• Sauté meats and vegetables in fat free chicken broth or water instead of oil. Fat free beef or vegetable broths also work well for sautéing.

• Chew gum while cooking. This will let you catch yourself taking a bite of this and that every time you remove the gum from your mouth.

• Drink cold water when cooking. You will have a much fuller feeling more quickly when it is time to eat.

• Experiment cooking with vinegars. These add zip to a wide variety of foods. I recommend trying balsamic and rice vinegars.

• Keep on hand jams, jellies, and zero fat candy for when the sweet tooth strikes.

Jalapeño Corn Bread

Servings: 6   Fat Grams: 1

1/2 c. egg substitute
1/4 c. applesauce
4 sliced jalapeños, finely chopped
1 (9 oz.) can cream style corn
1/2 c. nonfat sour cream
1 c. yellow cornmeal
1/2 tsp. salt, optional
2 tsp. baking powder
2 c. Kraft fat free shredded Cheddar cheese

Preheat oven to 350 degrees. Coat a 9 inch baking pan well with cooking spray. Stir together egg substitute, applesauce, and jalapeños. Blend into egg mixture corn, sour cream, cornmeal, salt, baking powder, and cheese. Stir well. Pour batter into prepared baking pan. Bake in preheated oven for 1 hour. It is done when a toothpick inserted comes out clean.

Easy Banana Nut Bread

Yield: 1 loaf

Fat Grams: 4.0 in whole loaf without pecans 14.0 in whole loaf with pecans

1 c. sugar
1/4 c. applesauce
2 bananas (1 cup), mashed
1/2 c. egg substitute, slightly beaten
2 c. low fat biscuit mix (Pioneer)
2 T. pecans, chopped fine, optional

Preheat oven to 350 degrees. Coat loaf pan with cooking spray. Cream sugar and applesauce. Fold in mashed bananas and egg substitute. Stir well. Gradually stir in biscuit mix. Sprinkle pecans over batter and stir just until blended. Bake for 45 minutes or until toothpick inserted comes out clean. Remove from oven and let stand 10 minutes. Remove from pan and slice. Great served with I Can't Believe It's Not Butter Spray.

Applesauce Nut Bread

Servings: 10   **Fat Grams: 0 without nuts**
                           2.01 with nuts

1/4 c. egg substitute, beaten
1 c. applesauce
2 T. liquid Butter Buds
2 c. all-purpose flour
3/4 c. sugar
1 tsp. cinnamon
3 tsp. baking powder
1/2 tsp. soda
1 tsp. salt, optional
1/4 c. pecans, chopped fine, optional

Preheat oven to 350 degrees. Coat a 9 x 5 x 2-3/4 loaf pan with cooking spray. Combine egg substitute, applesauce and Butter Buds. Sift flour, sugar, cinnamon, baking powder, soda and salt together; add to egg mixture. Mix all ingredients well. Add the nuts to the batter. Pour into prepared loaf pan and bake for 45 minutes or until toothpick inserted comes out clean.

Zucchini Bread
"This bread gets better with age."

Yield: 2 loaves   **Fat Grams: 1.5 per loaf**

2 c. all-purpose flour
3/4 c. whole wheat flour
2 tsp. baking soda
1/2 tsp. baking powder
3 tsp. cinnamon
1/2 tsp. nutmeg
1 c. sugar
1 c. light brown sugar
1 c. applesauce or nonfat plain yogurt
3/4 c. egg substitute, beaten
3 tsp. vanilla
3/4 c. seedless raisins
2 c. grated zucchini

Preheat oven to 350 degrees. Coat two 4-1/2 x 9 inch loaf pans with cooking spray. Sift together both flours, baking soda, baking powder, cinnamon, and nutmeg into large bowl. Cream in separate bowl sugar, brown sugar, egg substitute, and vanilla. Add egg mixture to flour mixture. Stir just until moistened. Fold lightly into batter raisins and zucchini. Turn into prepared pans. Bake in preheated oven for 1 hour. Check for doneness by inserting toothpick in center of loaf. When done toothpick will come out clean.

Eggnog Bread

| Yield: 1 loaf | Fat Grams: 0 without pecans |
| (10 slices or servings) | 2.05 per slice with pecans |

3 c. all-purpose flour
1/2 c. sugar
4 tsp. baking powder
1/2 tsp. salt, optional
1/2 tsp. nutmeg
1/4 c. egg substitute
1-3/4 c. fat free eggnog
1/2 c. applesauce or nonfat plain yogurt
1/4 c. pecans, chopped, optional
1/2 c. golden raisins

Preheat oven to 350 degrees. Coat a 9 x 5 inch loaf pan. Stir flour, sugar, baking powder, salt, and nutmeg together. Combine egg substitute, fat free eggnog, and applesauce in small bowl. Add egg mixture to flour mixture. Blend in pecans and raisins. Pour into prepared loaf pan and bake for 1 hour. Note: If too much browning occurs, cover with foil for the last 10 minutes of baking time. Check for doneness by inserting toothpick in center of loaf. Loaf is done when toothpick comes out clean.

Cheddar Bread

Servings: 6   **Fat Grams: 1.11**

3-1/3 c. low fat biscuit mix (Pioneer)
or 0.5 grams of fat per 1/2 cup
2-1/2 c. Kraft fat free shredded Cheddar cheese
1/2 c. egg substitute
1-1/4 c. skim milk

Preheat oven to 350 degrees. Coat a 9 x 5 inch loaf pan with cooking spray. Blend together biscuit mix and cheese. Whip together egg substitute and skim milk. Add egg mixture to biscuit mix. Stir just enough to moisten. Bake in oven for 55 minutes.

Popovers

Servings: 8   **Fat Grams: 1.75**

1 c. sifted all-purpose flour
1/2 tsp. salt, optional
1/2 c. egg substitute
1 c. skim milk
1 T. vegetable oil

Preheat oven to 425 degrees. Coat muffin pan with cooking spray. Sift flour and salt. In a separate bowl beat the egg substitute with an electric mixer until eggs are light and thick. Add flour and 1/3 cup of the milk; continue to beat slowly until all the flour is moistened. Gradually add the remaining milk and oil; beat only until the mixture is free of lumps (about 1 to 2 minutes). Fill prepared muffin cups a little less than half full. Bake for 35 to 40 minutes or until the popovers are firm. Prick sides with toothpick to allow steam to escape so they will not become soggy. Serve immediately.

Whole Wheat Muffins

Servings: 18   **Fat Grams: .05**

1-1/2 c. whole wheat flour
1 c. all-purpose flour
1 tsp. baking powder
1 tsp. salt, optional
1 tsp. soda
1/4 c. applesauce or nonfat yogurt
1/2 c. sugar
1/2 c. egg substitute
1/2 c. low-fat buttermilk (1 fat gram per cup)
1/2 c. raisins

Preheat oven to 450 degrees. Coat muffin tin with cooking spray. Sift flours with each addition of baking powder, salt, and soda—three times. The last time sift into bowl. Cream applesauce, sugar, and egg substitute in a separate bowl. Beat until fluffy. Add buttermilk and flour mixture alternately to egg mixture. Stir just until blended after each addition. Add raisins and blend in with as few strokes as possible. Spoon batter into prepared muffin cups, filling two-thirds full. Place in preheated oven and bake for 20 minutes.

Oat Muffins

Servings: 15-18   **Fat Grams: .05**

1 c. low-fat buttermilk (1 fat gram per cup)
1 c. quick oats
1/4 c. egg substitute, beaten
1/2 c. brown sugar
1/3 c. applesauce or nonfat yogurt
1 c. flour
1 tsp. salt, optional
2 tsp. baking powder
1/2 tsp. soda

Combine buttermilk and oats in bowl. Cover. Refrigerate overnight. Preheat oven to 400 degrees. Coat muffin tin with cooking spray. Combine egg substitute, brown sugar, and applesauce with oat mixture. Stir lightly. Sift flour, salt, baking powder, and soda together. Add flour mixture to oat mixture. Stir just until moistened. Fill muffin cups two-thirds full. Bake in preheated oven for 20 minutes.

Bran Muffins
"Think Fiber"

Servings: 12   **Fat Grams: 0.13**

3/4 c. wheat bran
1/2 c. skim milk
1/2 c. maple syrup
1/4 c. egg substitute
1/4 c. applesauce or nonfat plain yogurt
1-1/2 c. whole wheat flour
1 T. baking powder
1/2 tsp. salt, optional
1/2 c. Grape Nut cereal (replaces nuts)

Preheat oven to 400 degrees. Coat muffin tin with cooking spray. Mix together bran, skim milk, and maple syrup. Stir in egg substitute and applesauce. In a separate bowl combine flour, baking powder, and salt. Add bran mixture to flour mixture. Stir just until moistened. Sprinkle in grape nuts. Stir lightly. Fill prepared muffin cups two-thirds full. Bake in preheated oven for 18 to 20 minutes.

Glaze

1 T. fat free margarine
1/2 c. confectioner's sugar
1 T. maple syrup

Combine all ingredients and stir. Spread glaze over warm muffins. Eat and enjoy being healthy!

Million Dollar Muffins

Servings: 12   Fat Grams: 0.63

1-1/2 c. all-purpose flour
2-1/2 tsp. baking powder
1/4 tsp. salt, optional
1 c. oat bran
1/2 c. light brown sugar, firmly packed
1 c. skim milk
1/3 c. applesauce or nonfat plain yogurt
1/2 c. egg substitute, slightly beaten
1 tsp. vanilla extract
1 (3 oz.) pkg. nonfat cream cheese, cut into 12 pieces
3/4 c. jam (your choice—try apricot)

Preheat oven to 425 degrees. Coat muffin tin with cooking spray. Sift flour, baking powder, and salt together. Add oat bran and brown sugar to flour mixture. Blend thoroughly; set aside. In separate bowl combine skim milk, applesauce, egg substitute, and vanilla. Stir. Add egg mixture to flour mixture. Stir just enough to moisten flour. Batter should be lumpy. Spoon batter into each cup one-half full. Add 1 T. jam on top of batter. Next place cream cheese on top of jam. Spoon remaining batter into each muffin cup. Bake in preheated oven for 14-16 minutes or until golden brown.

Hurry Up Muffins

Servings: 12   Fat Grams: 0

2 c. sifted self-rising flour
1 c. skim milk
1/4 c. Kraft fat free Miracle Whip salad dressing

Preheat oven to 400 degrees. Coat muffin pans with cooking spray. Place flour in a large mixing bowl. Add skim milk and salad dressing; stir until flour is just moistened. The batter will have a lumpy appearance. Fill prepared muffin pans two-thirds full. Bake for 20 minutes or until done.

Poppy Seed Muffins
"A Family Favorite"

Servings: 12   **Fat Grams: Less than 1**

1/2 c. low fat biscuit mix (Pioneer)
      or 0.5 grams per 1/2 cup
1/2 c. sugar
1 T. poppy seeds
1/4 c. egg substitute, beaten
3/4 c. nonfat sour cream
1 tsp. vanilla

Preheat oven to 400 degrees. Coat muffin tin with cooking spray. Combine biscuit mix, sugar, and poppy seeds into medium size bowl. Add beaten egg substitute, nonfat sour cream, and vanilla. Stir until just moistened. Let mixed batter stand for 20 minutes at room temperature before baking. Spoon into prepared muffin cups, filling half full. Bake in preheated oven for 20 minutes.

Apple-Raisin Muffins

Servings: 12   **Fat Grams: 0**

1-3/4 c. all-purpose flour
1/4 c. sugar
2-1/2 tsp. baking powder
3/4 tsp. salt, optional
1/2 tsp cinnamon
1 c. tart, crisp apples, peeled, chopped
1/4 c. raisins
1/4 c. egg substitute
3/4 c. skim milk
1/3 c. applesauce or nonfat plain yogurt

Preheat oven to 400 degrees. Coat muffin tin with cooking spray. Combine together flour, sugar, baking powder, salt, cinnamon. Stir well. Add to flour mixture apples and raisins. Stir well. Form well in center of flour mixture. Add to well egg substitute, skim milk, and applesauce. Stir just until moistened. Batter should be lumpy. Fill prepared muffin cups two-thirds full. Bake in preheated oven for 20 to 25 minutes. When done muffins should be golden brown.

Blueberry Buttermilk Muffins

Servings: 12   Fat Grams: 0

2 c. sifted all-purpose flour
1/2 c. sugar
1/2 tsp. salt, optional
1/4 t. baking soda
2-1/4 tsp. baking powder
1/4 c. liquid butter buds
1/4 c. egg substitute
1 c. low fat buttermilk (1 fat gram per cup)
1 c. blueberries

Preheat oven to 425 degrees. Coat muffin tins with cooking spray. Sift flour, sugar, salt, baking soda, and baking powder. In a separate bowl combine egg and buttermilk; stir well. Add egg mixture to the flour mixture. Stir just enough to moisten well. Fold in the blueberries. Fill prepared muffin cups about two-thirds full. Bake for 25 minutes.

Apricot Muffins

Servings: 12   Fat Grams: 1.68
Without pecans: trace of fat

2 c. all-purpose flour
4 tsp. baking powder
1/2 tsp. salt, optional
1/4 c. sugar
1/4 c. egg substitute
1/4 c. applesauce or nonfat plain yogurt
1 c. skim milk
1/4 c. pecans, chopped, optional
    (measure, then chop)
1/4 c. dried apricots, diced

Preheat oven to 400 degrees. Coat muffin tin with cooking spray. Sift flour, baking powder, salt, and sugar together. Add apricots. Mix in separate bowl egg substitute, applesauce and skim milk. Add to flour mixture. Lightly stir batter. Batter should be lumpy. Fill prepared muffin cups two-thirds full. Bake in preheated oven for 25 minutes. Use I Can't Believe It's Not Butter Spray and enjoy them warm.

Breakfast
& Beverages

"What lies behind us and what lies before us are tiny matters compared to what lies within us."

— **Emerson**

Eating Out - Car Travel - Motel Stays

Eating out, car travel, and staying in motels can cause undue stress when trying to lose weight. Here are some helpful tips that will allow you to have fun and stop worrying.

• **Plan Ahead.** If you know you are going out to dinner, compromise your eating and reduce intake during the day.

• **Menus.** When ordering from a menu, ask a lot of questions about how certain items are prepared. Also ask for a chart of menu items that list fat grams and calories. This will astound you. Avoid items that are deep fat fried, oily sauces, and heavy creams. Go for broiled, baked, or grilled entrees. Ask for salad dressing on the side and no butter on baked potatoes. Drink lots of water with the meal.

• **Buffet Blues.** Sing that tune no more. Walk the entire buffet first. Get your choices in mind. Begin with a salad. Eat slowly and stick to your choices for the main course. Remember it takes the brain 20 minutes to register a full feeling. Drink lots of water throughout the meal. For dessert if the choices are unfavorable get a plate of fresh fruit and ask for a small bowl of whipped cream to dip them in. More often than not, the restaurant will accommodate you.

• **Car Travel.** Plan for this just as you plan for taking along foods to keep small children happy. Keep a cooler of fresh fruits, vegetables, and zero fat dips. Pack low fat bread and lunchmeats, low fat chips, muffins, bagels, cookies, etc. Take plenty of water! Practice portion control and enjoy the trip.

• **Motel Stays.** Plan to stay at motels that offer a continental breakfast. Usually they offer low fat cereals, fruit, juice, coffee, bagels, and a toaster so you can toast your low fat bread. Since it is there and you've paid for it, you will be more likely to eat breakfast there instead of going out to eat where temptation lies. Remember to practice portion control.

Egg and Bacon Casserole

Servings: 8   Fat Grams: 4

1-1/2 c. egg substitute
3 c. skim milk
1/2 tsp. dry mustard
salt and pepper to taste, optional
12 slices low fat white bread (1 gram of fat per 2 slices)
16 oz. Kraft fat free shredded Cheddar cheese
1 lb. turkey bacon, cooked crisp, crumbled
**   (2.5 fat grams per slice)**
3 c. corn flakes, crushed
1/4 c. liquid Butter Buds

Coat a 9 x 13-inch baking dish with cooking spray. Whisk egg substitute, skim milk, dry mustard, salt and pepper. Layer in prepared baking dish bread, cheese, crumbled bacon, and sliced mushrooms, ending with a layer of bread on top. Pour egg mixture over bread. Cover with plastic wrap and refrigerate for 2 hours before baking. Thirty minutes before baking, combine crushed corn flakes and liquid butter buds. Preheat oven to 325 degrees. Just before baking, sprinkle corn flake mixture on top of casserole. Bake uncovered for 1 hour.

Egg and Cheese Casserole

Servings: 6   **Fat Grams: Less than 1**

1/4 c. all-purpose flour
1/4 c. liquid Butter Buds
1/8 tsp. black pepper
1 c. egg substitute
1 c. fat free cottage cheese
1 c. Kraft fat free shredded Cheddar cheese
1 (4 oz.) can diced green chiles, drained
1 (2 oz.) jar diced pimiento, drained
2 slices turkey bacon, cooked crisp, crumbled

Preheat oven to 375 degrees. Coat a 10 x 6 x 2-inch baking dish with cooking spray. Mix together flour, liquid Butter Buds, and pepper. Add to flour mixture egg substitute, cottage cheese, cheddar cheese, chiles, and pimientos. Stir well. Pour into prepared baking dish. Bake uncovered for 25 minutes or until set and slightly puffed. Sprinkle bacon on top and serve.

Breakfast Pizza

Servings: 8   **Fat Grams: 1.88**

1 (12 oz.) pkg. ground turkey sausage, crumbled
1/2 c. onion, chopped
1/2 c. green bell pepper, chopped
salt and pepper to taste, optional
1 T. corn oil
3 c. frozen fat free hash browns (Ore Ida)
3/4 c. egg substitute
1/2 c. skim milk
2 c. Kraft fat free shredded Cheddar cheese

Cook sausage, onion, and bell pepper in a large non-stick skillet. Drain using a colander. Rinse with hot water to remove excess fat. (Rinse skillet and dry thoroughly.) Heat oil in non-stick skillet. Press hash browns in bottom of skillet. Whisk together egg substitute and skim milk; pour over hash browns. Sprinkle sausage mixture on top of egg mixture and top with fat free Cheddar cheese. Cook on medium to low heat for 35 minutes or until eggs are set. Serve with salsa and nonfat sour cream.

Veggie and Cheese Omelet

Servings: 3   **Fat Grams: 2.33**

1 c. egg substitute
1/4 c. skim milk
salt and pepper to taste, optional
1/2 c. zucchini, coarsely chopped
1/3 c. tomato, chopped
1 T. onion, chopped
1/2 c. reduced fat shredded Monterey Jack cheese
chunky salsa
nonfat sour cream

Stir together egg substitute, skim milk, salt and pepper. Coat a large non-stick skillet with cooking spray. Heat skillet over medium heat. Pour a little more than 1/4 cup of egg mixture into skillet. Reduce heat to low. Cook until egg mixture is set and lightly brown on bottom. Sprinkle zucchini, tomato, onion, and reduced fat cheese over egg mixture. Fold omelet in half and cook for a few more seconds to melt cheese. Top with salsa and nonfat sour cream.

Breakfast Burrito

Servings: 4   Fat Grams: 1.3

1 c. egg substitute
2 T. skim milk
2 T. green bell pepper, diced
4 slices turkey bacon cooked crisp
**   (2.5 fat grams)**
4 (12-inch) fat free flour tortillas
1 c. Kraft fat free shredded Cheddar cheese

Scramble together egg substitute, skim milk, and green pepper. Follow this order to form each burrito. Scrambled egg mixture, slice of bacon and 1/4 cup cheddar cheese. Tuck in the ends and roll. Heat in microwave on HIGH for 30 seconds or until cheese melts. Serve with salsa and nonfat sour cream.

Zero Fat Pancakes

Servings: 8   **Fat Grams: 0**

1/2 c. egg substitute
1-1/2 c. skim milk
2 T. liquid Butter Buds
2 c. all-purpose flour, sifted
3 tsp. baking powder
1/2 tsp. salt, optional
1 T. sugar

Mix egg substitute, skim milk, and liquid butter buds. Sift together flour, baking powder, salt, and sugar. Add egg mixture to flour mixture. Beat only until smooth. Let stand for 10 minutes. Coat heated griddle with cooking spray. Pour by ladle onto hot griddle. Bake until bubbles on top of pancake burst open. Turn and bake on other side.

Note: To create fruit pancakes such as blueberry, apple, or banana, simply add 1 cup of fruit to batter. The fruit adds no fat to the pancake.

Banana-Cinnamon French Toast

Servings: 3   Fat Grams: 1

6 slices low fat white bread (1 gram of fat per 2 slices)
1/2 c. egg substitute
1/2 c. skim milk
1/2 tsp. cinnamon
1 banana, halved
powdered sugar

Place in blender egg substitute, skim milk, cinnamon, and banana halves. Pureé. Pour into medium size bowl. Coat griddle with cooking spray. Coat both sides of bread with banana mixture. Brown on both sides. Sprinkle powdered sugar on top of each slice.

Orange Honey Syrup

Yields: 1-3/4 cups   Fat Grams: 0

1-1/4 c. honey
1/3 c. orange juice
1 T. liquid Butter Buds
1/4 tsp. grated orange peel

Combine all ingredients in saucepan. Cook over medium heat, stirring constantly. Cook just until syrup is well-blended. Yummy!

Breakfast In Arkansas

When I was a child, my mom would take her mother to visit her parents, my great grandparents, Joe and Ruby Davis in Hardy, Arkansas. My brother and I called them Grandma and Grandpa Arkansas.

Off the beaten path surrounded by huge shade trees sat my great-grandparents' stone house. Off to the west of the house stood a large red barn where Grandpa milked his cow. Grandpa always met us at the wooden gate where he welcomed us every year. I can still remember the sound the gate made as it shut against the large post that supported it. After going through the gate, we walked up a stone walk-way that led us to the large front porch where Grandma stood adorned in her apron. She always gave strong hugs, the kind that made a kid feel loved.

In their house were two kitchens, a summer kitchen for when days were hot and a winter kitchen for those cold winter mornings. I also remember in the early years going to the outhouse. Now to a city kid that was a big deal. I guess that's why it stands out to me to this day.

I remember the great conversations that took place in Grandma's winter kitchen while she never missed a beat churning her butter. The smells from her cooking and her laugh still fill my head. At Grandma and Grandpa's house we got up early, before dawn. I recall waking to the sounds of Grandma stoking the old wood cook stove. From that stove came mountain high homemade biscuits, fried squirrel, thick juicy bacon, picture-perfect eggs, and wonderful gravy. To a kid who loved to eat it was like waking up in heaven. The table was heavily dressed with homemade blackberry jelly and a bowl of Grandma's churned butter.

We sat there long after breakfast just visiting. My grandpa liked to have his coffee served in a cup. Then he would pour it into a saucer that he would drink from. I never grew tired of watching him do that. I must admit I have tried Grandpa's technique of drinking coffee and I still haven't figured out how he did that. Grandma and Grandpa are gone now and I miss that special place in Arkansas, but the conversations and the laughter that took place around the breakfast table live on. Those kinds of memories never die.

As you might have guessed by now, down home cooking was the heart of our family. I feel I have succeeded in keeping Great-grandma's down home appeal—only without the fat!

Hooray! Biscuits
"Who says you can't have your biscuits and eat them too?"

Servings: 18 (2-inch) diameter,   **Fat Grams: 0**
1/4 inch thick dough
9 (1-inch) diameter,
1/2 inch thick dough

2 c. self-rising flour
1/3 c. nonfat sour cream
1 c. skim milk

Preheat oven to 450 degrees. Coat 9 x 13 x 2-inch baking pan with cooking spray. Make a well in flour and pour milk and nonfat sour cream into center of well. Stir quickly with fork. Dough will be sticky. Turn onto lightly floured surface. Roll, coating all sides with flour. Knead 6 times. Cut biscuits with 2-inch cutter, then place in prepared pan. (Cut out as many biscuits as possible the first time.) Gather all trimmings; do not knead. Flatten with palm of hand and cut remaining biscuits. Place in pan and bake in preheated oven for 12 to 15 minutes. Note: Halfway through baking time brush generously with liquid Butter Buds for a buttery golden crust or use Wesson butter flavor cooking spray.

Apple Biscuits

Servings: 16   Fat Grams: 0.5

1 c. Wheat Chex, crushed
1/2 c. grated unpeeled apples
1/2 c. apple juice
2 c. low fat biscuit mix (Pioneer) or
**   0.5 fat grams per 1/2 cup**
1/8 tsp. nutmeg
1/8 tsp. cinnamon

Preheat oven to 450 degrees. Coat cookie sheet with cooking spray. Combine in large mixing bowl cereal crumbs and grated apples. Pour apple juice over cereal mixture. In a separate bowl mix together biscuit mix, nutmeg, and cinnamon. Combine dry ingredients with cereal mixture. Mix thoroughly. Drop well rounded spoonfuls onto prepared cookie sheet. Bake in preheated oven for 10 minutes.

"Good Mornin'" Raisin Bread

Servings: 10   **Fat Grams: 0**

1 c. seedless raisins
1 c. boiling water
2 tsp. baking soda
1 c. sugar
1/4 c. egg substitute
1 T. fat free margarine
2 c. all-purpose flour

The night before you wish to serve them, pour boiling water over raisins and soda. Let mixture soak overnight. Do not drain. The next morning preheat oven to 325 degrees. Coat one loaf pan with cooking spray. Add to raisin mixture sugar, egg substitute, fat free margarine, and flour. Mix well. Pour batter into prepared loaf pan. Bake in preheated oven for one hour.

Glazed Apple Cinnamon Rolls

Servings: 12   **Fat Grams: 0**

3 c. all-purpose flour
2 T. baking powder
1 tsp. salt, optional
2 T. sugar
1/2 c. applesauce
1 c. + 2 T. skim milk
3 T. liquid Butter Buds
3/4 c. brown sugar, packed
3-1/2 c. tart apples, peeled and chopped
1/2 c. raisins
3 T. lemon juice
2 tsp. cinnamon

Preheat oven to 450 degrees. Coat jelly roll pan with cooking spray. Sift flour, baking powder, salt, and sugar. Stir in applesauce. Pour all of the skim milk into flour mixture. Stir batter just until moistened. Knead 10 times and roll out on lightly floured surface to one-fourth-inch thickness. (Dough should be oblong in shape.) Brush with liquid butter buds. Combine in bowl apples, raisins, lemon juice and cinnamon. Toss to coat. Spread apple mixture over top of dough. Sprinkle with brown sugar and roll up in jelly-roll fashion. Using a sharp knife, cut roll in one-inch slices. Place cut rolls on prepared pan. Bake in 450 degree oven for 10 minutes, then reduce to 350 degrees for another 25 minutes.

Glaze

1 T. liquid Butter Buds
2 T. lemon juice
1 c. powdered sugar

Combine in small bowl and stir. Drizzle over slightly cooled rolls. Enjoy.

161

Apple Coffee Cake

Yields: 2-9 x 9 cakes   **Fat Grams: 6.06 per cake**

1 c. brown sugar
1 c. sugar
1 c. all-purpose flour
1/2 c. fat free margarine
1 tsp. cinnamon
2 T. pecans, chopped fine
1/4 c. apples, peeled and diced
1/2 c. egg substitute
1 c. all purpose flour
1 c. low fat buttermilk (1 fat gram per cup)
1 tsp. baking soda

Preheat oven to 350 degrees. Coat two 9 x 9-inch cake pans with cooking spray. Blend together brown sugar, sugar, one cup of the flour, and fat free margarine. Remove one cup of this mixture and set aside. To the remaining mixture add cinnamon, pecans, and apples. Set aside. To the original mixture add egg substitute, flour, low fat buttermilk, and baking soda. Stir well. Divide cake batter equally between pans. Cover each cake with apple-pecan mixture. Bake in preheated oven for 30 minutes.

Breakfast Shake for Two

Servings: 2   Fat Grams: 0

1/4 c. orange juice concentrate
1 c. skim milk
2 tsp. sugar
1 ripe banana

Combine all ingredients in blender or food processor. Blend until smooth and creamy. Note: Grape juice concentrate can also be used.

California Gold

Servings: 6   Fat Grams: 0

1 (16 oz.) can cling peach slices or halves in juice
1/4 tsp. cinnamon
3 c. skim milk
1 c. fat free peach yogurt

Combine peaches and cinnamon in blender or food processor; puree. Add to peach mixture milk and yogurt. Blend well. Pour into pitcher for easy serving.

Concord Buttermilk Shake

Servings: 2   **Fat Grams: .5**

1 c. low-fat buttermilk (1 fat gram per cup)
1/2 c. fat free vanilla ice cream
1/2 c. concord grape juice
2 T. brown sugar
1 T. orange flavored drink mix (Tang)
orange slices

Combine all ingredients in blender or food processor. Blend on high until smooth and creamy. Garnish with orange slices.

Coffee Cooler

Servings: 4   **Fat Grams: 0**

4 c. fresh strong coffee, cooled
4 sm. scoops fat free vanilla ice cream
2 T. sugar
6 ice cubes

Place all ingredients into blender. Blend until smooth and creamy. Serve immediately.

Orange Soda

Servings: 4   Fat Grams: 0

**1/2 c. orange juice
2 tsp. lemon juice
2 T. sugar
2 tsp. skim milk
1/2 c. diet lime soda
2 large scoops fat free vanilla ice cream**

Place all ingredients into pitcher. Mix slightly. Stir in 1/2 cup diet lime soda. Serve immediately.

My own secret dreams, wishes and commitments to myself.

(Make several blank copies of this page and as you progress update your dreams, wishes and commitments.)

_____

_____

_____

_____

_____

_____

_____

_____

_____

_____

_____

_____

_____

_____

_____

_____

_____

Desserts

"Life itself is the proper binge."
— **Julia Child**

Low Fat Baking & Freezing Tips

• Cake mixes can be made successfully by substituting applesauce for cooking oil and using egg substitute instead of whole eggs. (1/4 of cup egg substitute for each egg called for.)

• Substitute canned, evaporated skim milk when a recipe calls for heavy whipped cream. Remove top lid of can and set can in freezer. Partially freeze until ice crystals lightly form on top. At the same time place mixing bowl and beaters in freezer. Whip until light and fluffy. You will have great results if you follow these instructions.

• When using measuring cups or spoons, lightly spray them with cooking spray first before adding nonfat margarines, honey, etc. The ingredients will slide right out.

• For perfect meringue, use room temperature egg whites.

• For a delicious fat free icing for cup cakes, place a large marshmallow on each cup cake. Place in microwave oven for a few seconds to melt. Also, try sprinkling powdered sugar on top of cake, cupcakes, or muffins instead of icing.

• Don't throw out over-ripe bananas. Mash and freeze them. Use when baking breads, muffins, cookies, etc. Bananas serve to replace the oil called for in recipes.

• To freeze cookie dough for later use, stuff dough into an empty can. (Make sure the bottom can be cut open.) When ready to use, cut open can bottom and push dough out. Slice with a large cheese slicer and bake.

• To prevent chicken breasts from sticking together when freezing, try this. Remove skin and all visible fat. Lay each piece on a jelly roll pan, making sure they don't touch. Freeze. When frozen, remove and place serving size portions in freezer-safe zip lock bags. To safely thaw chicken, either use microwave on defrost setting or place on bottom shelf of refrigerator. This method also works well with turkey patties and other meats.

Sour Cream Apple Pie

Servings: 16   **Fat Grams:**   **With Walnuts: 4.55**
Without Walnuts: 4.0

1 unbaked 8-inch pastry shell
   (4 fat grams per serving)
1/2 c. egg substitute
1/2 c. sugar
2 T. all-purpose flour
1/4 tsp. salt, optional
1 T. lemon juice
1 c. nonfat sour cream
4 c. tart apples, peeled and sliced thin

Crumble Topping

1/4 c. all-purpose flour
1/4 c. firmly packed brown sugar
1/8 c. walnuts, chopped
1/2 tsp. cinnamon
1/8 tsp. salt
3 T. nonfat margarine

Preheat oven to 400 degrees. Combine egg substitute, sugar, flour, salt, and lemon juice. Stir well. Fold in sour cream. Evenly place apple slices in pastry shell. Pour sour cream mixture over top of apples. To make topping combine flour, sugar, walnuts, cinnamon, and salt. Stir. Add nonfat margarine to flour mixture. Using tines of fork, blend until mixture resembles course crumbs. Evenly sprinkle crumb mixture over top of pie. Bake in preheated oven for 35 to 40 minutes. Variation: Use equal amounts of fresh peaches instead of apples.

Billy Bob's Blackberry Pie

My husband loves blackberries. According to Bill,
"I never met a blackberry I didn't like."

Servings: 16   **Fat Grams: 4**

1 c. sugar
1 (3 oz.) box blackberry gelatin (or grape)
4 T. cornstarch
2 c. water
4 c. blackberries
1 (9-inch) baked pie shell
   (4 grams fat per serving)
fat free Cool Whip topping/fat free vanilla ice cream

Combine sugar, gelatin, cornstarch, and water in sauce-pan. Cook over medium heat until thick. Cool completely before stirring in blackberries. Spoon into baked pie shell. Serve with fat free Cool Whip or fat free vanilla ice cream.

Lemon Meringue Pie

Servings: 6-8   **Fat Grams: 2**

Crust
**3/4 c. lowest fat graham cracker crumbs
(choose lowest fat graham crackers)
1 T. sugar
3 T. liquid Butter Buds**

Crush graham crackers by placing them in a large ziplock bag. Roll with rolling pin to crush. Mix crumbs, sugar, and liquid Butter Buds together in 8 or 9-inch pie plate. Press mixture firmly in bottom and up sides.

Filling
**1 c. sugar
3 T. cornstarch
1-1/2 c. boiling water
1 T. liquid Butter Buds
juice of 1 lemon or 3 T. lemon juice
grated rind of 1 lemon, optional
3/4 c. egg substitute**

Combine sugar, cornstarch, and water in saucepan. Over medium heat cook for 2 minutes stirring constantly. Add liquid Butter Buds, lemon juice, lemon rind, and egg substitute to sugar mixture and whisk vigorously. Cool. Spoon filling into crust.

Meringue
**3 egg whites at room temperature (very important!)
6 T. sugar**

Preheat oven to 425 degrees. Beat egg whites and sugar with electric mixer on high until stiff peaks form. (approximately 10 minutes) Spread evenly over filling using spatula to dab and lift meringue for pretty peaks. Bake in preheated oven for 4 to 5 minutes or just until meringue is lightly brown.

Cody's Unforgettable Double Chocolate Pie

This was created for my son Cody-my "chocolate buddy."

Servings: 16   **Fat Grams: 2.25**

1 (15 oz.) pkg. brownie mix
   (Use egg substitute and replace oil with
   applesauce)
1 (5.8 oz.) box instant chocolate pudding
2 c. skim milk
1 (20 oz.) can cherry pie filling
1 can nonfat whipped topping

Preheat oven to setting required on brownie mix. Coat a 12-inch pizza pan with butter flavor cooking spray. Prepare brownie mix following package directions. Spread batter on pizza pan. Form a crust edge with batter. Bake in preheated oven. Cool. Mix pudding with skim milk, using 1 cup less than package directions. Spread pudding over cooled brownie crust. Leave a 1/2-inch edge around crust. Spread cherries over pudding, saving one for garnish. Chill for 1 hour. Just before serving decorate edge with canned whipped topping. Form a circle in the center with whipped topping and place cherry on top.

"This recipe never goes begging at the Collins' house or at family get-togethers!" Enjoy.

Pineapple Ice Cream Pie
"Cool and refreshing on a hot day!"

Servings: 6   **Fat Grams: 2**

1 (3 oz.) box lemon gelatin
1 c. hot water
1 pt. fat free vanilla ice cream
1 (16 oz.) can crushed pineapple, drained
2 T. of reserved pineapple juice
1 graham cracker crust, chilled
(See Lemon Meringue Pie for recipe.)

Combine gelatin with hot water. Stir to dissolve gelatin. Fold in fat free ice cream. Stir until ice cream has melted. Add pineapple and juice. Refrigerate until partially thickened. Spoon into chilled crust. Return to refrigerator until set. Enjoy!

Pecan Pie

Servings: 16   **Fat Grams: 5.28**

1 c. egg substitute, beaten (Hiland)
1 c. brown sugar
1 c. light corn syrup
1/4 c. pecans, chopped fine
1 unbaked pie crust
   (Use brand with 4 fat grams per serving.)

Preheat oven to 425 degrees. Combine egg substitute, brown sugar, and corn syrup. Blend well. Pour into unbaked pie crust. Sprinkle pecans on top, using a spoon to push them into filling mixture. Bake in 425 degree oven for 5 minutes, then reduce temperature to 300 degrees. Continue baking for 1 hour (watch closely) or until set and knife inserted comes out clean.

Note: Measure pecans out in halves, then chop in food processor. You will have enough to cover entire pie. (Reason - you will consume less fat this way than if you measured out 1/4 cup already chopped.) The pie will rise high above crust while baking. This is normal. Once removed from oven it will go down.

Lemon Cheesecake

Servings: 6   Fat Grams: 1

1 (8 oz.) pkg. nonfat cream cheese, softened
2 c. skim milk
1 (3.4 oz.) pkg. lemon pudding mix
1 (9-inch) graham cracker pie crust
(See Lemon Meringue Pie for recipe)
1 (21-oz.) can cherry pie filling

Blend nonfat cream cheese with one-half cup skim milk using fork. Add remaining skim milk and pudding mix to cream cheese mixture. Beat on low with electric mixer for one minute. Do not overbeat. Pour into graham cracker crust. Chill for 30 minutes. Spread cherry pie filling over top and chill for 30 minutes longer.

Luscious Pineapple Cake

"So pretty, so good. This is always a hit at family get-togethers."

Servings: 12   **Fat Grams: 2 without pecans**
                          With pecans: 3.26

1 (18 oz.) box yellow cake mix
   (Prepare cake mix using egg substitute and
   applesauce for oil.)
1 (8 oz.) pkg. nonfat cream cheese
1/2 c. skim milk
1 (3.4 oz.) box fat free instant vanilla pudding
1 c. skim milk
1 (20 oz.) can crushed pineapple, drained,
   reserve 1/4 c. liquid
1 (9 oz.) carton fat free Cool Whip topping
2 T. pecans, chopped, optional
2 T. maraschino cherries, drained, rinsed, and coarsely
chopped

Preheat oven according to cake mix directions. Coat cake pan with cooking spray. Replace eggs with egg substitute and oil with applesauce. Bake and cool cake completely. Combine nonfat cream cheese with one-half cup skim milk. Beat with electric mixer until smooth. There will be small bits of unblended cream cheese, but this is normal. Beat pudding and one cup skim milk into cream cheese mixture until thickened. Let stand for 10 minutes. Brush reserved juice over entire cake. Cake should be moist, not soggy. Spread pudding mixture over cooled cake. Sprinkle drained, crushed pineapple over pudding mixture. Evenly spread fat free Cool Whip on top of pineapple. Refrigerate for 4 hours. Just before serving sprinkle with chopped pecans and maraschino cherries.

Fruit Cocktail Cake
"Soo Luscious"

Servings: 10   Fat Grams: 1.22

1 (16 oz.) can fruit cocktail in lite syrup
1/2 c. egg substitute
1-1/2 c. sugar
2 c. flour
2 tsp. baking soda
2 tsp. baking powder
1 tsp. salt, optional

Preheat oven to 350 degrees. Coat a 13 x 9 x 2-inch cake pan with cooking spray. Combine fruit cocktail with juice and egg substitute in large bowl. Sift dry ingredients together. Combine dry ingredients with fruit mixture. Stir well. Pour batter into prepared pan. Bake in preheated oven for 1 hour. Icing should be hot and ready to pour on cake as soon as it comes out of the oven.

Coconut Icing

1 c. sugar
1/2 c. coconut (6 fat grams per 1/4 cup)
1/2 c. liquid butter buds
1 (14-1/2 oz.) can evaporated skim milk
1 tsp. vanilla

Combine all ingredients in saucepan and bring to boil. Make holes in warm cake. Pour hot frosting over cake as soon as it is removed from the oven.

Fruit Cocktail Cake
"Soo Luscious"

Servings: 10   **Fat Grams: 1.22**

1 (16 oz.) can fruit cocktail in lite syrup
1/2 c. egg substitute
1-1/2 c. sugar
2 c. flour
2 tsp. baking soda
2 tsp. baking powder
1 tsp. salt, optional

Preheat oven to 350 degrees. Coat a 13 x 9 x 2-inch cake pan with cooking spray. Combine fruit cocktail with juice and egg substitute in large bowl. Sift dry ingredients together. Combine dry ingredients with fruit mixture. Stir well. Pour batter into prepared pan. Bake in preheated oven for 1 hour. Icing should be hot and ready to pour on cake as soon as it comes out of the oven.

Coconut Icing

1 c. sugar
1/2 c. coconut (6 fat grams per 1/4 cup)
1/2 c. liquid butter buds
1 (14-1/2 oz.) can evaporated skim milk
1 tsp. vanilla

Combine all ingredients in saucepan and bring to boil. Make holes in warm cake. Pour hot frosting over cake as soon as it is removed from the oven.

Mock Poundcake
"Very moist and very easy to make!"

Servings: 12   Fat Grams: 1.5

**1 (18.25 oz.) yellow cake mix
1/3 c. nonfat sour cream
1 c. water
3/4 c. egg substitute
powdered sugar**

Preheat oven to 350 degrees. Coat two 9 x 5-inch loaf pans with cooking spray. Mix all ingredients with electric mixer on low for two minutes. Scrape sides of bowl. Turn mixer on high and mix for six to eight minutes longer. Batter is ready when pale colored peaks stand up when beaters are raised. Fill prepared loaf pans half full of batter. Bake in oven for 35 to 40 minutes. Cake will rise and crack on top. Let cool for five minutes. Dust with powdered sugar. (Place a cookie cutter in cake to make indentations before dusting with powdered sugar.) Remove from pan. Cool completely. Place on serving plates and cover with plastic wrap. (The purpose for wrapping in plastic wrap is it makes it super moist.) This recipe is great served with strawberries and nonfat Cool Whip.

Note: For a poppy seed pound cake, add 1 tablespoon of poppy seed to batter before baking.

Very Low Fat Chocolate Cake

Yields: 10 slices   **Fat Grams: 0.5 per slice**

2 c. all-purpose flour
1 c. sugar
4 T. cocoa
1 tsp baking powder
1 tsp. baking soda
1 c. Kraft fat free Miracle Whip salad dressing
1 c. cold water
1 tsp. vanilla
powdered sugar

Preheat oven to 350 degrees. Coat a 11 x 7 shallow loaf pan with cooking spray. Sift together flour, sugar, cocoa, baking powder, and baking soda into large mixing bowl. Add salad dressing, cold water, and vanilla. Beat for two minutes on medium speed of electric mixer, scraping sides frequently. Pour into prepared loaf pan and bake in oven for 30 to 35 minutes or until inserted toothpick comes out clean. Sprinkle top with powdered sugar.

Grandma's Sugar Cookies

As a child there was nothing I enjoyed more than curling up in my grandparents' feather bed on a cool morning. I loved to snuggle down under the covers just leaving my head out; it seemed Grandma's laundry always smelled so good.

The memory that stands out most was an early morning spring rain. I can still hear the noise from the old screen door as it banged shut signaling Grandma's return from turning her chickens out. And before I knew it, I heard the familiar sound of Grandma making my favorite cookies on her old baking cupboard. My brother and I usually got to help make cookies, but on this particular day we did not because Grandma knew how much we loved to sleep in when it was raining.

I remember how the window in the bedroom was raised just enough to let the cool breeze in. The rain was steadily falling and I could hear it making a puddle just below the window. I would lay there very still listening to the eggs crack on the side of the bowl and the flour bin being pulled open on the cupboard.

I remember how fascinated I was the many times I watched Grandma use a wad of this and a pinch of that to make her perfect cookie dough. I am not sure if she even had a recipe to follow. I just remember her hand serving as her measuring cup. By the way her cookies turned out, it was a very accurate way to measure.

Grandma knew how much I loved to eat her raw cookie dough. I could always count on a large piece wrapped in wax paper and placed in the refrigerator just for me. (A practice I would no longer recommend.)

Those are memories from my childhood that bring a smile to my face every time my boys and I make sugar cookies.

Grandma's cupboard has retired to the wash house now. It serves proudly as a plant stand in the winter. The paint is cracked and peeling and it looks a little sad. But when I look at its cracked and peeling paint that is not what I see. I see a cupboard where a grandma and her two grandkids had fun in the kitchen making sugar cookies and lots of memories.

My wish was to be able to create fond memories with my boys when it came to making sugar cookies. My No Roll Sugar Cookie recipe allows me to do just that—guilt free.

No Roll Sugar Cookies
(Can be rolled)

**Yields: 3-4 dozen   Fat Grams: 0 per cookie without icing
Trace with low-fat icing**

1 c. sugar
1 c. nonfat margarine or unsweetened applesauce
1/4 c. powdered sugar
1/4 c. egg substitute, Hiland (fat free)
1 tsp. vanilla
1/4 tsp. lemon flavoring
2 1/2 c. flour
1 tsp. soda
1 tsp. cream of tartar
sugar
Pillsbury *lowest fat* icing

Preheat oven to 350 degrees. Lightly coat cookie sheet with butter flavor cooking spray. Cream together sugar, nonfat margarine, powdered sugar, egg substitute, vanilla, and lemon flavoring. Sift together flour, soda, and cream of tartar. Stir into cream mixture. Drop by teaspoonful onto prepared cookie sheet. Dip flat bottom glass in sugar and flatten each cookie. Bake in preheated oven for 10 to 12 minutes or until edges are slightly brown.

Note: To roll out cookie dough simply place on floured surface, knead in just enough flour to stiffen the dough. Roll. Use cutters of choice. Bake just until set, but not brown around edges. Top with icing and colored sugar toppings.

For best results store baked cookies in airtight container.

This recipe is dedicated to my Grandma Conn. Thanks for my many wonderful childhood memories.

Almond Butter Cookies
"Light and Wonderful"

Yields: 3 dozen   **Fat Grams: 0**

1 c. nonfat margarine
1 tsp. almond extract
1/2 c. sugar
2 c. self-rising flour
sugar

Preheat oven to 350 degrees. Lightly coat cookie sheet with butter flavor cooking spray. Cream together nonfat margarine, sugar, and almond extract. Stir in flour. Form one-inch balls; roll in sugar. Place cookie on prepared cookie sheet and flatten with a large spoon. Bake for 12-15 minutes until edges are slightly brown.

Oatmeal Crunchies

Yields: 4 dozen   **Fat Grams: 0**

1/2 c. all-purpose flour
1/4 c. sugar
1/2 tsp. baking powder
1/2 tsp. baking soda
1/4 tsp. salt, optional
1/4 c. brown sugar
1/4 c. nonfat margarine
1/4 c. egg substitute
2 T. nonfat plain yogurt
1/4 tsp. vanilla
1 c. quick-cooking rolled oats

Sift together flour, sugar, baking powder, baking soda, and salt into large mixing bowl. To flour mixture add brown sugar, margarine, egg substitute, yogurt, and vanilla. Beat well using a wooden spoon. Stir in oats. Chill dough for 1 hour. Drop cookies by teaspoonful on ungreased cookie sheet. Bake at 375 degrees for 8 minutes or until slightly golden brown. Cool for 2 minutes before removing from cookie sheet.

Chocolate Chip Cookies

Yields: 8 dozen 2" cookies   **Fat Grams: Less than 1 per cookie**

1 c. sugar
1 c. brown sugar
1 c. nonfat margarine, room temperature
3/4 c. egg substitute
1 tsp. vanilla extract
3 c. all-purpose flour
1-1/2 tsp. baking soda
pinch salt, optional
1/2 c. semi-sweet chocolate chips

Preheat oven to 400 degrees. Coat cookie sheet with butter flavor cooking spray. With electric mixer on low beat sugar, brown sugar, margarine, egg substitute, and vanilla. Set aside. Combine flour, soda, salt. Stir well. Add flour mixture to creamed mixture. Stir well. Add chocolate chips. Drop by teaspoonful on prepared cookie sheet. Bake in oven for 8 to 10 minutes. Cool for 2 minutes before removing from cookie sheet.

This recipe is dedicated to my 15-year-old nephew Cory, whose famous words are, "Got any more?"

Chocolate Pudding Cookies

Yields: 36 cookies   **Fat Grams: Less than 1
per cookie**

1 (3 oz.) pkg. fat free instant chocolate pudding
3/4 c. low fat biscuit mix (Pioneer)
    (0.5 fat grams per 1/2 cup)
1/4 c. applesauce
1/4 c. egg substitute

Preheat oven to 350 degrees. Line baking sheet with parchment paper. Combine all ingredients in bowl. Blend until firm. Form into one-inch balls and place on prepared baking sheet. Flatten with tines of fork. Bake in preheated oven for 8 to 10 minutes.

Variation: Make an ice cream sandwich by placing fat free vanilla ice cream between 2 cookies. Very low in fat! Enjoy.

Raisin Bars

Yields: 12   **Fat Grams: 0**

1 c. raisins
2 c. water
1/2 c. liquid Butter Buds
1 c. sugar
1 tsp. baking soda
1 tsp. cinnamon
1-3/4 c. flour
1/2 tsp. nutmeg
1/4 tsp. salt, optional

Bring raisins to boil in 2 cups of water. Add liquid Butter Buds; cool. Preheat oven to 350 degrees. Coat a 7 x 11-inch pan with butter flavor cooking spray. Sift together sugar, soda, cinnamon, flour, nutmeg, and salt. Stir in raisin mixture. Pour into prepared pan. Bake in preheated oven for 20 to 30 minutes.

Brown Sugar Brownies

Yields: 35 squares

**Fat Grams: 3.5 in entire recipe
With Pecans: 1.15 per brownie**

**6 T. liquid Butter Buds
2 squares chocolate, melted
1/2 c. egg substitute
2 c. brown sugar
1 c. all-purpose flour
1/4 tsp. salt, optional
1/2 tsp. vanilla
1/2 c. chopped pecans, optional**

Melt chocolate with liquid Butter Buds in top of double boiler over low heat. Preheat oven to 275 degrees. Coat a 9 x 13-inch pan with butter flavor cooking spray. Beat egg substitute. Add all remaining ingredients. Stir well. Spread into prepared pan. Bake for 30 minutes in preheated oven. Cool. Cut into squares.

Peach Crisp

Servings: 8   Fat Grams: 0

3/4 c. all-purpose flour
2 T. oatmeal
3/4 c. brown sugar
1/4 tsp. salt, optional
1/2 tsp. cinnamon
1/3 c. nonfat margarine
3 c. fresh peaches, peeled and sliced
(other fruits may be used)

Preheat oven to 350 degrees. Coat 8-inch square baking dish with cooking spray. Combine flour, brown sugar, salt, and cinnamon. Stir to blend. Cut in nonfat margarine with fork until crumbly. Place peaches in prepared baking dish. Sprinkle crumb mixture over peaches. Bake for 40 to 45 minutes or until golden brown. Great served with fat free vanilla ice cream.

Blueberry Bu

Servings: 6-8   **Fat G**

1/4 c. nonfat margarine
3/4 c. sugar
1/4 c. egg substitute
1-1/2 c. all-purpose flour
2 tsp. baking powder
1/2 tsp. salt, optional
1/2 c. skim milk
2 c. blueberries

Topping

1/2 c. sugar
1/3 c. all-purpose flour
1/2 tsp. cinnamon
1/4 c. nonfat margarine
nonfat vanilla ice cream

Preheat oven to 350 degrees. Coat a 8 x 8-inch baking pan with butter flavor cooking spray. Cream nonfat margarine, sugar, and egg substitute. Set aside. Sift together flour, baking powder, and salt. Add sifted dry ingredients alternately with skim milk. Fold in blueberries. Stir just until blended. Pour into prepared pan. Using a fork stir together topping ingredients until mixture forms crumbs. Sprinkle topping over batter. Bake in preheated oven for 40 minutes. Serve warm with nonfat vanilla ice cream. Yummy!

Strawberry Delight

Servings: 8   Fat Grams: 0 in filling
Check pastry shells for lowest fat content.
"Read those labels."

1 (9-inch) dessert shell (resembles a large shortcake)
1/3 c. orange juice
1/2 c. nonfat sour cream
1 (8 oz.) carton fat free Cool Whip, thawed
1 pt. strawberries, hulled
1/3 c. strawberry jelly, melted
fresh mint leaves

Brush entire cake layer with orange juice. Combine nonfat sour cream and 2-1/2 cups of Cool Whip. Use a wire whisk to blend thoroughly. Spread Cool Whip mixture evenly over entire cake. Arrange strawberries with top sides down. Start in middle of shell working towards the outside. Brush melted jelly over top of strawberries. Garnish center with mint leaves. Chill for 1 hour before serving.

Note: Do not overblend nonfat sour cream; it will cause it to break down to a liquid.

Strawberry Cream Cheese Pizza

Servings: 16   Fat Grams: 1.5

1/4 c. low fat graham cracker crumbs
1 (8 oz.) pkg. nonfat cream cheese, softened
3/4 c. sugar
1/2 c. egg substitute
1 c. fat free Cool Whip topping
1 pt. (2 c.) strawberries
(Other fruits may be used)
1 (8 oz.) carton fat free Cool Whip topping

Sprinkle low fat graham cracker crumbs over bottom of 9-inch springform pan. Combine cream cheese and sugar. Using electric mixer beat until light and fluffy. Add egg substitute, one-fourth cup at a time. Beat well after each addition. Fold in fat free Cool Whip. Pour into springform pan. Place in freezer for 4 hours or overnight. Remove sides of pan. Arrange sliced strawberries on top. Cut into wedges. Garnish with fat free Cool Whip.

Strawberry Yogurt Medley
"Cool and Refreshing"

Servings: 8   **Fat Grams: 0**

1 (3 oz.) pkg. nonfat cream cheese, softened
2/3 c. strawberry nonfat yogurt
2 tsp. sugar
2 c. fresh strawberries, halved
2 med. oranges, peeled and sectioned
1 lg. banana, bias-sliced
nonfat Cool Whip

Beat cream cheese until smooth with electric mixer. Fold in nonfat yogurt and sugar. Chill well. When ready to serve, prepare fruit and place in serving bowl. Pour cream cheese mixture in middle of fruit. Top with nonfat Cool Whip.

Bread Pudding

Servings: 4   Fat Grams: 1 for entire recipe

1/2 c. egg substitute
2-1/4 c. skim milk
1 tsp. vanilla
1/2 tsp. ground cinnamon
1/4 tsp. salt, optional
2 slices low fat bread, cut into 1-inch cubes
      (Wonder, 1 fat gram per 2 slices)
Land O' Lakes fat free half-and-half

Preheat oven to 350 degrees. Coat a 8-1/4 x 1-3/4-inch round cake pan with butter flavor cooking spray. Combine egg substitute, milk, vanilla, cinnamon, and salt. Stir in bread cubes. Add sugar. Mix well. Pour mixture into prepared baking pan. Place this pan in a larger pan with 1 inch of water in it. Bake in a preheated oven for 35 minutes or until knife inserted in center comes out clean. Serve warm with half-and-half.

Angel Butterscotch Pudding

Servings: 4-6 **Fat Grams: 0**
With pecans: 2.53

1/4 angel food cake, cut into 1-inch cubes
1 (3.4) oz. pkg. fat free butterscotch pudding mix
(Do not use instant!)
2 c. skim milk
2 T. pecans, toasted and chopped, optional
fat free Cool Whip topping

Arrange angel food cake cubes in bottom of 8-inch square serving dish. Cook pudding with skim milk following package directions. Pour hot pudding over cake cubes. Sprinkle with toasted pecans. Serve warm with fat free Cool Whip.

Noodle Pudding

Servings: 8   **Fat Grams: 1**

1 (16 oz.) pkg. Yolk Free wide egg noodles, cooked and
     drained
1/2 c. nonfat sour cream
1/2 c. nonfat cottage cheese
1/2 c. nonfat cream cheese mixed with 1/2 tsp.
     cornstarch (prevents nonfat cream cheese from
     separating during baking)
1 c. sugar
1 tsp. cinnamon
1-1/2 tsp. salt, optional
1-1/2 tsp. vanilla
1 c. egg substitute, beaten
1 (20 oz.) can crushed pineapple, drained
1/2 c. raisins
1/4 c. liquid Butter Buds
1 c. skim milk

Preheat oven to 350 degrees. Coat a 13 x 9-inch pan with
butter flavor cooking spray. Combine all ingredients
except milk in mixing bowl. Stir well. Turn into
prepared bowl. Stir well. Pour into prepared pan. Pour
skim milk over noodle mixture. Bake in preheated oven
for 1 hour.

Quick Custard

Servings: 6   **Fat Grams: 0**

1 c. egg substitute
1/4 c. sugar
1 tsp. vanilla extract
3 c. skim milk
nutmeg
6 custard cups

Beat egg substitute slightly. Add remaining ingredients to egg mixture and beat well. Arrange filled custard cups in large deep skillet with a tight fitting lid. Pour hot water in skillet to 1-inch below rim of custard cups. Bring to full boil; cover skillet immediately. Turn heat off. Let stand for 8 minutes (Do not peek!) Remove custard cups. Let cool, then sprinkle nutmeg. After cooling to room temperature place in refrigerator.

Note: To check for doneness, insert sharp knife in center of custard. If done the knife will come out clean.

Kids' Cuisine, Etc...

"Never let the fear of striking out get in your way."
— **George Herman "Babe" Ruth**

Low Fat Ideas for Kids of All Ages

• Zero fat pita bread makes for easy delicious pizza crust. My kids favorite is "Mexican Pizza." Spray bottom of pita bread with I Can't Believe It's Not Butter Spray; lightly sprinkle garlic salt, optional, on top. Place on broiler shelf and toast. Turn over, spread one-half cup fat free refried beans and one-fourth cup Kraft fat free shredded cheddar cheese. Broil until cheese melts. Top with tomato or lettuce and tomato and nonfat sour cream. Delicious and zero fat.

• Pita chips are easy and fun to make. Cut whole pita bread in half, then cut into wedges. Separate. Spread out on cookie sheet. Bake at 350 degrees for 10 minutes or just until lightly brown. Zero Fat. Use just like chips. Can also spray with Wesson butter flavor cooking spray and lightly sprinkle with garlic salt, optional.

• Fat free flour tortillas are a wonderful way to use leftovers. Try fat free mashed potatoes with fat free cheese rolled in the tortilla. Rice, chicken, fat free cheese, salsa can be rolled in a tortilla, heated, and topped with nonfat sour cream.

• Try baked potatoes topped with steamed broccoli and melted fat free Healthy Choice process cheese. Fat free chili and fat free shredded cheddar cheese and nonfat sour cream are also good. Try lean roast beef and fat free gravy.

A Lesson Learned

As I recall, it was early November, the leaves had fallen, the air was cold, and there were many walnuts that needed to be picked up on my grandparents' farm.

I was nine and my brother was seven. I remember Grandpa Conn explaining to us that all we had to do was fill a five gallon bucket full of walnuts and then take them to the nut house to be sold. As a result of the sale, I would get the money from my bucket of walnuts. Now being a kid all that registered to me was getting some money. I did not think about or realize the work involved in filling the bucket.

On the way to the walnuts, I remember thinking about how much fun I was going to have spending my money at the Yellow Front store in Coffeyville, Kansas.

When we arrived, Grandpa handed me my bucket. To my amazement the bucket looked nothing like the one we used to help Grandma gather her eggs. Why, this thing was huge.

The "fit" began. I started whining about how I would never be able to fill such a thing. All I could think about was how much work it was going to be. Mom and Grandma told me to sit my bucket in the middle of the walnuts so I could easily pick them up and drop them in. For this nine-year-old that was just too much work.

I came up with a better plan on how I could get done quicker. When no one was looking I robbed handfuls of walnuts out of everyone's bucket and put them in mine.

My plan was going great, but then I made the biggest mistake of all; my little brother caught me. He began to scream, telling everyone what I was doing. I remember Grandpa explaining to me that if I wanted the money I would have to work for it.

As it turned out the walnuts were returned including those belonging to my screaming little brother. I did succeed in picking up my own walnuts that day. It seemed as if it would take forever, but my bucket eventually was filled. I was able to buy the monkey with the banana in its hand at the Yellow Front store with my hard-earned walnut money.

My grandpa Conn is gone now and I miss his wisdom. When dealing with my own children's pains of growing up, I'm glad to be blessed with memories of lessons taught to me by grandpa . . . it's those little lessons that I learned in my childhood, that make being Cody, Jake and Wyatt's mom so rewarding.

Thank You, Grandpa!

Fun Time Taco Platter

Servings: 4 **Fat Grams: 1**

1 lb. ground turkey breast
1 envelope taco seasoning
1 (8 oz.) bag baked low fat tortilla style chips
1/2 small head lettuce, shredded
1 large tomato, diced
1 (8 oz.) pkg. Kraft fat free shredded cheddar cheese
salsa

Caution: When operating stove, children should have adult supervision!

Brown ground turkey in non-stick skillet. Drain in colander. Rinse with water. Rinse out skillet. Return meat to skillet. Add taco seasoning and one-fourth cup water. Cook over low heat until bubbly hot. Arrange chips on platter. Top chips with meat, lettuce, tomato, and cheese. Garnish with salsa if desired. Let the kids dig in. (It's a great way to get kids to eat fresh vegetables!)

This entire kid section is dedicated to my niece Kelly who can really decorate a pretty table and to my nephew "Chef" Kevin who can cook a mean cake. To my son Jake for his stupendous Saturday morning breakfast and last but not least to Wyatt for his "Giant" masterpiece biscuits.

Wyatt's Mini Pizzas
According to my youngest son Wyatt,
"They're just good!"

Servings: 4   Fat Grams: 1

2 English muffins, split
4 T. zero fat spaghetti sauce
1/2 c. Kraft fat free Mozzarella cheese

Caution: When operating oven, children should have adult supervision!

Preheat oven to broil. Place English muffin halves on broiler pan. Spray each with I Can't Believe It's Not Butter Spray. Toast in broiler. Spread one tablespoon spaghetti sauce on each toasted muffin. Sprinkle equal amounts of cheese over top. Broil just until cheese melts. If you're like Wyatt, they will disappear fast.

Note: You can also use leftover cooked vegetables or lowfat sandwich slices for pizzas.

Mini Fruit Cheese Cakes

Servings: 8   Fat Grams: 3

1 (8 oz.) pkg. nonfat cream cheese with pineapple
1 c. powdered sugar
2 tsp. lemon juice
8 individual dessert cakes
2 c. berries or cut up fresh fruit
(try blackberries, peaches, and kiwi)
fat free Cool Whip topping

Caution: When children are using knives and electric mixers, adult supervision is recommended.

Combine cream cheese, powdered sugar, and lemon juice. Mix well. Place wax paper on cookie sheet. Arrange dessert cakes on paper. Spread sides and top of each cake with cheese mixture. Chill until serving time. When ready to serve, place 1/4 c. of berries or fresh fruit on top. Garnish with a tablespoon of fat free Cool Whip topping.

Gooey Marshmallow Treats or Pizza

**Yield: 25 to 30 squares Fat Grams: 0 for
2 square-serving**

1/4 c. liquid Butter Buds
5 c. miniature or 45 large marshmallows
5 c. crispy rice cereal

Coat jelly roll pan with butter flavor cooking spray. Combine liquid Butter Buds with marshmallows in microwave safe bowl. Microwave for 1-1/2 minutes or just until the marshmallows melt. Remove from microwave and stir for a few more seconds to fully melt marshmallows. Mix in cereal. Press into prepared jelly roll pan. Cool, cut into squares.

Note: Press into prepared pizza pan. Let children decorate pizza with gummy bears or other fat free or low fat toppings. Fun to do at birthday parties.

Some-More Sandwich Treat
My kids' famous words "give me some more"
hence the name.

Servings: 2   Fat Grams: 1.5

2 reduced fat whole graham crackers
2 large marshmallows or marshmallow cream (1 tsp.) for each
1 tsp. reduced fat fudge icing

Break graham cracker in half. Lay one marshmallow in middle of graham cracker. Place on broiler safe pan. Place in broiler just until marshmallow lightly browns. Spread one-half teaspoon fudge icing on other half of the graham cracker. Squash together. Enjoy.

Caution: When operating broiler, children should have adult supervision!

Note: When using marshmallow cream do not place in broiler.

Fun to do at birthday parties!

Gingerbread Men
"Kids of all ages love these!"

Yields: 5 dozen   **Fat Grams: 3.68 per cookie**

1 c. vegetable shortening
1 c. sugar
1 c. dark molasses
3/4 c. egg substitute
1 T. white vinegar
6 c. all-purpose flour
2 tsp. baking soda
1 tsp. salt, optional
1 tsp. ginger
1 tsp. cinnamon

Caution: When operating electric mixer and oven, children should have adult supervision.

Cream shortening and sugar together until fluffy with electric mixer on medium speed. Blend in molasses, egg substitute, and vinegar. Mix well. In separate bowl sift together flour, soda, salt, ginger, and cinnamon. Stir flour mixture into molasses mixture until well blended. Wrap in plastic wrap. Chill until dough is firm (about 1 hour). Preheat oven to 375 degrees. Lightly coat cookie sheet with cooking spray. Divide dough in half. Roll dough out on lightly floured board to one-fourth inch thickness. Cut with floured cookie cutter gingerbread men or women. Place on prepared cookie sheet and bake in preheated oven for 12 to 15 minutes. Cool on wire racks. After cookies are cool, decorate with icing by outlining features and clothing.

Note: Decorative frosting may be iced after baking or raisins for gingerbread man's eyes and buttons may be placed on before baking.

Decorative Icing
for Gingerbread Men

1 T. vegetable shortening
1 lb. confectioner's sugar
1 tsp. vanilla
3 to 4 T. skim milk

Cream shortening with electric mixer. Add sugar, vanilla, and 2 tablespoons of the milk. Beat well. Add more milk to obtain desired consistency for use in decorating tube.

Popsicles

Servings: 10   **Fat Grams: 0**

Dry Mix

2 (0.15 oz.) pkg. Kool Aid
1 (3 oz.) pkg. gelatin
(Gelatin should be the same flavor as Kool Aid.)
1-3/4 c. sugar

Mix all ingredients together and store in plastic container in refrigerator.

Making Popsicles

6 T. dry mix
3/4 c. hot water

Stir well to completely dissolve mix. Add 3/4 cup cold water. Stir again. Pour into popsicle molds. Freeze and enjoy.

Fudgesicles

Servings: varies with mold size   **Fat Grams: 0**

1 box instant nonfat chocolate pudding
1/2 c. sugar
3 c. hot skim milk (at boiling point)

Caution: When handling hot milk, children should have adult supervision.

Combine pudding and sugar in bowl. Slowly stir in hot milk. Mix well. Pour into molds. Freeze and enjoy.

Frozen Peanut Butter-Chocolate Covered Bananas
"Fun to make and eat!"

Servings: 2   Fat Grams: Trace

1 large ripe banana, cut in half
2 tsp. peanut butter
    (Peter Pan Smart Choice Reduced Fat)
3 T. Hershey's chocolate syrup
2 popsicle sticks
1/2 c. Grape Nuts, Rice Krispies, or Honey Nut Cheerios

Coat small plate with butter flavor cooking spray. Mix together peanut butter and chocolate sauce. Set aside. Spread cereal on a plain plate. Set aside. (Now comes the fun!) Insert popsicle stick into cut end of banana. Brush on chocolate mixture. Roll in cereal. Place on prepared plate and put in freezer for 2 hours. Enjoy.

Salt Dough
Cookie Cutter Ornaments
(Non-edible)

1 c. salt
2 c. all-purpose flour
1 c. water
nail (to punch hole)

Combine salt and flour in bowl. Stir in water, a little at a time. Knead for 8 to 10 minutes or until firm. Roll dough out on a clean surface until one-fourth inch thick. Use favorite cookie cutter shapes. Punch a hole in tope of ornament with the nail. Bake on cookie sheet in 325 degree oven for 30 minutes or until hard.

Caution: When operating oven, children should have adult supervision.

After baking, ornaments are now ready for paint and varnish. (Get help with the varnish from Mom or Dad). Tie a ribbon or string through the hole to finish the ornament. These make wonderful gifts for teachers and relatives.

Fun Dough
Non-edible
("This is a great way for kids to pass time on a rainy day!
Kids love it!")

1 c. flour
1/2 c. salt
2 tsp. cream of tartar
2 T. cooking oil
1 c. water

Combine dry ingredients in a large saucepan. Add oil and water. Stir over medium heat. Cool, Knead well. Store in an air-tight container.

Caution: When cooking, children should have adult supervision.

Variation: Add food color. Knead. The food color will stain hands until well blended, so use plastic gloves. Old clothes or aprons are recommended for this project. That includes you too, mom.

Potato Necklace
(Not recommended for wear by kids under age 6.)
Mom, you will want to make these for yourself.

2 potatoes, peeled and cubed in thumb-size pieces
Bamboo skewers
Foam
Acrylic paint, Apple Barrel
Clear enamel spray paint
Elastic string
Round beads

Caution: When using knife and paint, children should have adult supervision.

Place potato cubes on skewers, leaving good air space between each one. When skewer is filled, place in foam. Repeat process until all potatoes are used. Place on a shelf for one week. Every other day, twist potato cubes to loosen on skewer. Potatoes will be dark gray in color and very hard after one week. Now for the fun part! For a turquoise necklace paint potatoes on skewers turquoise blue. Let dry. Lightly sponge black paint over this. Wipe off most as you would if you were antiquing wood. Place skewer in foam to allow paint to dry. After paint dries, spray each piece with clear enamel. Again place skewer in foam to dry. When "stones" are thoroughly dry, remove them from skewer. Measure elastic to correct size for easy removal over head and cut elastic to length desired for necklace. Alternate placing "stones" and silver beads on necklace until it is full. Tie knot in string. Wear your new jewelry and fool everyone. Kids can create their own special color combinations. Super fun!

Hot Fudge Topping

Yields: 1 cup   **Fat Grams: 3.5 in entire recipe**

1/2 c. sugar
3 T. cocoa
1/2 c. boiling water
1-1/2 T. cornstarch
pinch of salt, optional
1 T. liquid Butter Buds
1 tsp. vanilla

Combine sugar, cocoa, water, cornstarch, and salt in double boiler. Stir until thick. Stir in liquid Butter Buds and vanilla. Serve over fat free ice cream. Enjoy. Store in covered container in refrigerator.

Caramel Sauce

Yields: approximately 3 cups   **Fat Grams: 0**

1 c. brown sugar
6 T. water
1/4 tsp. soda
1 c. Karo syrup
1 T. liquid Butter Buds
2/3 c. evaporated skim milk

Combine brown sugar, water, soda, syrup, liquid Butter Buds in double boiler. Boil until soft ball stage. Turn off heat. Stir in evaporated skim milk. Enjoy over fat free ice cream. Store in covered container in refrigerator.

Zero Fat Popcorn Seasoners

Yields: 8 cups popcorn   **Fat Grams: 0**

Cinnamon Butter Seasoning

1/4 c. liquid Butter Buds, warmed
1 T. cinnamon sugar

Garlic Butter Seasoning

1/4 c. liquid Butter Buds
1/2 tsp. garlic salt or garlic powder

Lemon Butter Seasoning

1/4 c. liquid Butter Buds
1 T. lemon juice

To coat popcorn, drizzle a small amount of seasoning on popcorn. Toss and repeat process until all seasoning has been used. Enjoy.

Orange Butter

Yields: approximately 1 cup   **Fat Grams: 0**

1/2 c. fat free margarine (Ultra Promise)
1 T. orange juice
1 tsp. orange peel, grated fine

Whip together with fork until smooth. Serve on warm bread or muffins. Store in refrigerator.

Substitutions

There is nothing more aggravating than to find out you don't have all the ingredients you need to complete your recipe! Don't despair, these substitutions work quite well.

Ingredient	Substitution
1 T. cornstarch	2 T. flour
1 cup sifted all-purpose flour	1 c. plus 2 T. sifted cake flour
1 cup sifted cake flour	1 c. minus 2 T. sifted all-purpose flour
1 tsp. baking powder	1/4 tsp. baking soda + 1/2 tsp. cream of tartar
1 cup milk	1/2 cup skim evaporated milk + 1/2 cup water
1 cup buttermilk	1 cup skim milk + 1T. white vinegar or lemon juice
1 cup sour cream	1 cup fat free yogurt + 1 T. cornstarch
1 cup plain yogurt	1 cup low fat buttermilk (fat free or 1 gram per cup)
1 tsp. dry mustard	1 T. prepared mustard
1 sm. onion	1 T. instant minced onion
1 cake compressed yeast	1 pkg. or 2 tsp. active dry yeast
1 square chocolate	3 T. cocoa + 1 tsp. vegetable shortening
1 tsp. allspice	1/2 tsp. cinnamon + 1/8 t. ground cloves
1 T. fresh snipped herbs	1 tsp. dried herbs
1 lemon	3 T. or 1/4 c. lemon juice
1 cup honey	1-1/4 sugar + 1/3 c. water
1-1/2 cups corn syrup	1 cup sugar plus 1/2 tsp. soda
1 cup sugar	2/3 c. honey plus 1/2 tsp. soda
1 cup brown sugar	1/2 cup granulated sugar plus 1/2 cup molasses + 1/4 tsp. soda
1 whole egg to thicken	1/4 c egg substitute + 2-1/2 T. water
1 whole egg	1/4 c. egg substitute
1 cup nuts in baked goods	1/2 cup Grape Nuts cereal

Equivalent Chart

3 tsp	1 T.
2 T	1/8 cup
4 T	1/4 cup
8 T	1/2 cup
16 T	1 cup
5 T. + 1 tsp	1/3 cup
12 T	3/4 cup
4 oz.	1/2 cup
8 oz.	1 cup
16 oz.	1 lb.
1 oz.	2 T. liquid
2 cups	1 pt.
2 pt.	1 qt.
1 qt.	4 cups
5/8 cup	1/2 cup + 2 T.
7/8 cup	3/4 cup + 2 T.
1 jigger	1 - 1/2 fl. oz. (3 T.)
1 lb. butter	2 cups or 4 sticks
2 - 2/3 cups powdered sugar	1 lb.
2 - 2/3 cups brown sugar	1 lb.
4 cups sifted flour	1 lb.
4 - 1/2 cups cake flour	1 lb.
3 - 1/2 cups unsifted whole wheat flour	1 lb.
8–10 egg whites	1 cup
1 cup unwhipped canned skim milk	2 cups whipped
1 lb. shredded American cheese	4 cups
1 chopped med. onion	1/2 cups onion pieces
1 lemon	1 tsp. grated peel
1 lemon	3 T. juice
1 orange	1/3 cup juice
1 orange	2 tsp. grated peel
4 oz. (1 to 1 - 1/4 cups) uncooked macaroni	2 - 1/4 cups cooked
7 oz. spaghetti	4 cups cooked
4 oz. (1 - 1/2 to 2 cups) uncooked noodles	2 cups cooked
28 reduced sodium saltine crackers	1 cup crumbs
4 slices low fat bread	1 cup crumbs
14 squares low fat graham crackers	1 cup crumbs
22 low fat vanilla wafers	1 cup crumbs

Liquid Measure

Cups Spoons	Quarts Ounces
1 tsp	1/6 ounce
2 tsp	1/3 ounce
1 T	1/2 ounce
3 to 3 - 1/3 T	1 - 3/4 ounces
1/4 cup	2 ounces
4 T	2 ounces
1/3 cup	2 - 2/3 ounces
5 - 1/3 T	2 - 2/3 ounces
1/3 cup + 1 T	3 - 1/2 ounces
1/2 cup	4 ounces
8 T	4 ounces
1 cup	8 ounces
16 T	4 ounces
2 cups	1 pint
16 ounces	1 pint
2 cups + 2 - 1/2 T	17 ounces
4 cups	1 quart
32 ounces	1 quart
4 - 1/3 cups	1 quart, 2 ounces

Oven Tips

Greater Success will be achieved by placing your baking products on the proper shelf.

Top Shelf
Cookies
Pie Shells
Rule: Usually foods that bake in 12 minutes or less.

Middle Shelf
Cakes
Quick Breads
Bars
Casseroles
Rule: Usually foods that bake in 25 to 35 minutes.

Bottom Shelf
Roasts
Breads
Rule: Usually foods that bake 1 hour or more.

Oven Temperature

Very slow .... **250 degrees F.**

Slow .... **300 degrees F.**

Moderate .... **325 - 350 degrees F.**

Moderately hot .... **375 degrees F.**

Hot .... **400 - 425 degrees F.**

Very hot .... **450 - 500 degrees F.**

Can Size Chart

Although cans no longer read (e.g. No. 303), this chart gives a quick reference when converting your old favorite recipes to accommodate today's labels.

8 oz. can or jar .... 1 cup

10-1/2 oz. can (picnic can) .... 1-1/4 cups

12 oz. can (vacuum) .... 1-1/2 cups

14 - 16 oz. or No. 300 can .... 1-1/4 cups

16 - 17 oz. can or jar or No. 303 can or jar .... 2 cups

1 lb., 4 oz. or 1 pt., 2 fl. oz. or
    No. 2 can or jar .... 2-1/2 cups

1 lb., 13 oz. can or jar or No. 2-1/2
    can or jar .... 3-1/2 cups

1 qt., 14 fl. oz. or 3 lb., 3 oz., or 46 oz. can .... 5-3/4 cups

6-1/2 to 7-1/2 lb. or No. 10 can .... 12 - 13 cups

Index

Appetizers & Dips

Appetizers

Dips

Soups, Salads and Sandwiches

Salads

Soups

Sandwiches

Vegetables

Entrees and Side Dishes

Entrees

Side Dishes

Breads and Muffins

Muffins

Breakfast and Beverages

Breakfast

How To Order

To order additional copies of this cookbook, please return an order form along with your check or money order to:

Aspire Publishing
P.O. Box 392
Chelsea, OK 74016

I would like to order _____ copies of the *Low Fat and Happy Cookbook* at $11.95 per copy and $3.00 for shipping and handling per book. Enclosed is my check or money order for $_____.

Mail Books to:

Name _____

Address _____

City _____ **State** _____ **Zip** _____

- -

I would like to order _____ copies of the *Low Fat and Happy Cookbook* at $11.95 per copy and $3.00 for shipping and handling per book. Enclosed is my check or money order for $_____.

Mail Books to:

Name _____

Address _____

City _____ **State** _____ **Zip** _____